D0873624

The Zune
PocketGuide

Bart G. **Farkas**

*All the Secrets of the Zune,
Pocket Sized.*

**Peachpit
Press**

The Zune Pocket Guide
Bart G. Farkas

Peachpit Press
1249 Eighth Street
Berkeley, CA 94710
510/524-2178
800/283-9444
510/524-2221 (fax)

Find us on the Web at: www.peachpit.com
To report errors, please send a note to errata@peachpit.com

Peachpit Press is a division of Pearson Education

Editors: Clifford Colby and Kathy Simpson
Production editor: Connie Jeung-Mills
Compositor and illustrator: Owen Wolfson
Indexer: Rebecca Plunkett
Cover design: Aren Howell
Cover photography: Aren Howell
Interior design: Kim Scott, with Maureen Forys
Product images are courtesy of their respective companies.

ISBN 0-321-48980-2

9 8 7 6 5 4 3 2 1

Printed and bound in the United States of America

*This book is dedicated to my wife, Cori,
and my three great kids: Adam, Derek,
and Natasha. They are the reason.*

Acknowledgments

First off, I have to thank Kathy Simpson (the book's editor) for her fantastic help with the book and for putting up with me along the way. She's a rock, and the books I work on with her make me greatly indebted to her. I also want to thank Cliff Colby at Peachpit for bringing me on board as well as for his editing and idea-management prowess.

I need to thank my kids, who always suffer when I'm writing a book because I'm not as available to them as usual, but they do a great job of understanding. And I thank my wife, Cori, for running the show when I'm embedded in work.

I guess as a final thought, I should thank my two new cats, Mr. Bean and Pikachu, for being fuzzy, soft, cuddly, and indifferent.

About the Author

Bart G. Farkas is the author of more than 90 books, most of which are strategy guides for computer and video games, but he has produced a reasonable catalog of technology books as well.

A former registered nurse, pilot, musician, and petroleum transfer technician, he spends his time writing fiction and nonfiction books in the idyllic climes of Cochrane, Alberta, in the company of his wife, three children, and two cats.

Contents

Introduction

The Zune can be said to be just another digital media player attempting to take a bite out of Apple, which dominates the MP3 market (controlling nearly three-quarters of it as of this writing). But the fact is that with a company such as Microsoft backing it, the Zune might just be the product to bruise the nice shiny Apple.

Technological politics aside, the Zune (**FIGURE i.1**) is an impressive piece of equipment designed to fit right into the world of Windows/PC users who like to listen to music, podcasts, and audiobooks and even watch television shows and movies with a small media player.

Figure i.1
The Microsoft Zune digital media player.

This introduction covers what's in the Zune box and what you need to do to get up and running in the world of Zune. The rest of the book covers everything from the history of MP3 players to the Zune's feature list; it also tells you how to deal with the Zune software and accessories, and even how to hack the device to get it to work "outside the box."

Zune vs. iPod?

It's a safe bet that many folks who purchase the Zune are interested in getting away from the whole iPod community. In fact, looking at the Zune-related forums, message boards, and blogs, it is clear that there is significant anti-Apple/anti-iPod sentiment among Zune enthusiasts. For this reason, Zune fans are likely to be annoyed by comparisons between the Zune and the iPod, but with the iPod's market dominance, some comparisons are bound to occur.

Note that I'm not siding with or against the iPod or the Zune when I compare the two devices in this book. Rather, I'm merely comparing the industry standard (iPod) with the hot new kid on the block (Zune).

Open It Up!

This section shows you what's inside your Zune's box and what steps you need to take to get up and running with the Zune software on your Windows PC. This is not a detailed tutorial but a quick-and-dirty procedure to get you rolling with minimal muss and fuss.

1. Get inside the box

You paid the $249 (or whatever the current price is) and took the Zune home; now it's time to dive in and frolic in the crisp, exciting newness of this highly anticipated digital device. Let's have a look at what's inside the box (**Figure i.2**):

- The Zune itself is seated just under the flip-up lid. Pull on the cloth strap to extract the Zune.

- To the left of the Zune is the USB cable that connects the Zune to your PC.

- To the right of the Zune are the headphones and headphone socks (the little spongy covers that go over the in-ear portion of each headphone).

- The right side of the box contains a small flip-up flap, under which you'll find the software CD, start guide, and product guide (**Figure i.3**); a Zune Pass, good for a 14-day free trial of Zune Marketplace; and a slick carrying pouch for your new device.

Figure i.2
The just-opened
Zune box.

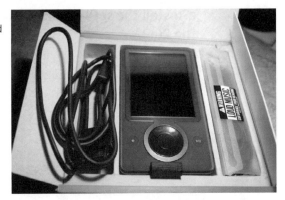

Figure i.3
The software/
information
folder.

2. Install the software and charge the Zune

The Zune is charged through the USB port of your computer, so charging the battery (which you should do first) involves connecting it to the computer. Begin by inserting the startup CD supplied with the Zune, and follow the onscreen directions to install the software. When you're prompted, connect your Zune to the PC and leave it to charge for at least a couple of hours. (Microsoft suggests charging for at least 3 hours.)

After you've installed the software, you can go ahead and put music, video, and pictures on your Zune.

Here's a breakdown of what comes preinstalled on your Zune.

Audio tracks

- The Adored, "Tell Me Tell Me"
- Band of Horses, "Wicked Gil"
- Bitter:Sweet, "The Mating Game"
- CSS, "Alala (Microsoft Edit)"
- Darkel, "At the End of the Sky (Microsoft Edit)"
- Every Move a Picture, "Signs of Life"
- The Rakes, "Open Book"
- Small Sins, "Stay"
- The Thermals, "A Pillar of Salt"

Music videos

- BT, "1.618"
- Chad VanGaalen, "Red Hot Drops"
- Coldcut (featuring Roots Manuva), "True Skool"
- CSS, "Let's Make Love and Listen to Death from Above"
- Fruit Bats, "The Wind Blew My Heart Away (Live)"
- Grandaddy, "Elevate Myself"
- Hot Chip, "Over and Over"
- Kinski, "The Snowy Parts of Scandinavia (Live)"
- Kraak & Smaak (featuring Dez), "Keep Me Home"
- Serena Maneesh, "Drain Cosmetics"
- Paul Oakenfold (featuring Brittany Murphy), "Faster Kill Pussycat"
- 30 Seconds to Mars, "The Kill"

Film shorts

- *A New York Skateboarding Minute* (skateboarding)
- *Kranked—Progression* (mountain biking)
- *The North Face* (skiing/snowboarding)

Pictures

- 12 posters from the Art of Modern Rock poster exposition

Beware the Sync!

Your Zune comes with quite a bit of sample music, video, and pictures on board right out of the box. That material is great to use to see just what your Zune is capable of, but beware: The first time you sync with your PC, all that material is erased from your Zune, and you cannot get it back!

Unfortunately, there's no way to avoid losing this material when you sync, so if you want to enjoy it, do so before you put your own files on the Zune.

3. Create a Zune account

Now it's time to go online with the Zune software and create an account for your Zune. For that, you need a Windows Live ID. If you don't already have one, you can create it by clicking the Create a New Account hyperlink in the Signing in to Zune dialog box (**FIGURE i.4**).

Figure i.4
Click the Create a New Account link to set up a new Windows Live ID.

To create the account, you need to enter a *Zune tag*: the name that the Zune community is going to see and know your Zune by. After you choose your name, go through the process of entering your personal information and setting up your account.

4. Sign in to your Zune account

When your account is up and running, you can remove the Zune startup disc from your PC, and you don't even have to have the Zune attached to your PC if you don't want to (although it's best if you do, so you can charge it). Now you need to sign in to your Zune account via the Sign In menu at the top of the Zune software page (**FIGURE i.5**). Signing in takes you to Zune Marketplace, where you can purchase points that you'll use to buy music, videos, and artwork (or pictures).

Figure i.5
With your Windows Live ID, sign in to your Zune account.

5. Redeem your prepaid code

Now you can go to the Add Microsoft Points page (**Figure i.6**), where you can purchase Microsoft Points (which are like money, because you use them to purchase media items, such as videos and music) or redeem the prepaid code that came with your Zune.

Figure i.6
Redeem your
prepaid code!

To get to this page, click the icon at the top that looks like a person's head and torso; then choose Account Summary from the menu. From this page, go to the Account Management area, and click the Zune Pass button in the Microsoft Points area.

You likely will want the free stuff, so enter the code on the back of your 14-day free pass from Microsoft to get yourself up and running in Zune Marketplace.

If you feel like purchasing some music from Zune Marketplace, feel free to do so now. When music is purchased, it's downloaded into your library automatically; you can synchronize it to your Zune later.

6. Rip a CD

If the preceding heading doesn't make sense to you, it's my duty to advise you that you are likely not jiggy with it. (That said, you shouldn't worry, because those of us born before 1985 find it difficult to get jiggy at all. In fact, just using this now-passé word shows that I'm not jiggy in the first place.)

Ripping a CD does not mean that you are damaging the disc in some way; rather, it means taking some or all of the songs/music/content on an audio CD and converting it to a digital format that your Zune player can read. In this case, you need only insert an audio CD into your computer's CD/DVD drive and watch it appear in your Zune software window.

To make your life even easier, your Zune software seems to know exactly what the CD is and what the songs on it are. (This technology is very cool, but you may run into problems when you put in custom-made audio CDs, because the software may not be able to tell what the song names are.)

Click the Start Rip button in the bottom-right corner of the Zune window, and watch your CD get ripped into your Zune library (**Figure i.7**) in a matter of minutes—usually fewer than 3 minutes, depending on your hardware.

Figure i.7
An album—in this case, Pottery Barn's *Margarita Mix*—is being ripped into my Zune library.

Start/Stop Rip button

7. Connect your Zune and synchronize

If you haven't already, connect your Zune to your PC and then synchronize it with the content you just purchased/ripped to your library. It's as easy as that!

After you have synchronized the music between your library and your Zune, you can listen to it on the Zune wherever you go (**Figure i.8**). You can use several variations when it comes to synchronizing; I cover them in detail in Chapter 3.

Figure i.8
The Zune's synchronization status appears in the top-right section of the Zune window.

8. Create playlists

If you want to organize your digital content in some way other than by artist, album, or genre, click the Create and Edit Playlists button in the top-right corner of the Zune software. To place songs in a playlist, you need only drag them to it. When the songs are in the playlist, the number of songs and the amount of time they take to play are displayed in the top-right corner (**FIGURE i.9**). At this point, you can synchronize again to place the playlists on your Zune (if you want).

Figure i.9
Create a playlist, if you are so inclined.

You can create as many playlists as you want, the advantage being that you can group music into special categories that you can tell your Zune to play or shuffle from. This ensures that you hear exactly the music or other audio files that you want to hear.

9. Disconnect the Zune, and enjoy

You don't have to do anything special to disconnect
the Zune other than pull the USB cable out from
the side of it. If you are actively synchronizing a
large amount of content, of course, you don't want
to disconnect the Zune, but otherwise, just pull the
cable off.

When the Zune is free of its umbilical cord to your
PC, plug in the headphones, and start listening!

Meet the Zune

The Zune is Microsoft's carefully constructed response to Apple's iPod devices, which dominate the market. In fact, some research shows that Apple controls more than 75 percent of the entire digital media player market, and its iTunes Store is definitely the big daddy when it comes to selling music online, with more than a billion (that's 1,000,000,000) songs sold and counting.

The Zune comes in with many of the same features as the 30 GB iPod. That is:

- It has a color screen.

- It holds 30 GB of data.

- It has an input device on the front. (The iPod has a scroll wheel, and the Zune has buttons that look like a wheel.)

- It connects to a PC via a USB port.

- It can play music and video as well as display pictures.

- It can connect to an online marketplace that sells media in digital format.

This chapter takes a look at what the Zune is capable of and what all the fuss is about.

A Brief History of Digital Media Players

Otherwise known as MP3 players, digital media players can trace their roots to the old Sony Walkman–style cassette players that dominated the portable-audio market in the late 1970s and throughout the 1980s. The Walkman spurred competitors to create smaller and cheaper players with added benefits, such as built-in radios, and when the Compact Disc (CD) format came into its own in the late 1980s, the market responded with a bevy of tiny CD players. This trend continued into the '90s with MiniDisc players (by Sony) and other similar devices, but the limitations of this technology—namely, storage space and battery life—were starting to annoy consumers, who demanded huge leaps in technology that the industry couldn't provide with CDs, tapes, and MiniDiscs.

In the mid-1990s, MP3 showed up. MP3, which stands for MPEG-1 Audio Layer 3, soon became the standard for digital audio compression worldwide. By 1998, the MP3 format was being used to play music on PCs with the help of a piece of software called WinAmp, and it was at this time that the first viable MP3 players came onto the scene.

Early MP3 players were flash-memory machines, capable of holding only 64 MB of data, but by late 1999, hard-drive MP3 players started to appear, offering hundreds of megabytes of storage space.

The market for MP3 players was fragmented until the winter of 2001, when Apple Computer released the first iPod (**FIGURE 1.1**) to a mixed response. The iPod turned out to be special, however, and it's estimated that more than 70 million of the devices have been sold worldwide, catapulting Apple to the front of the digital-media-player market.

Figure 1.1
A modern Apple iPod.

Courtesy of Apple Computer

note

MPEG stands for *Moving Picture Experts Group*, which was established in 1988 to set standards for digital encoding. The MPEG compression algorithms were developed at the University of Erlangen in Germany by Dieter Seitzer and by Karlheinz Brandenburg at a company called Fraunhofer-Gesellschaft.

Enter the Zune

Released on November 14, 2006, the new Zune created a huge buzz, with many people feeling it is the only media device that can stand up to Apple's iPod. There are two reasons for this opinion: the player's impressive feature list and the massive clout of Microsoft. When Microsoft launched the Xbox several years ago, going up against industry giants Sony and Nintendo, the game box didn't exactly set the world on fire, but now the Xbox 360 is a stellar machine that has put a dent in the highly competitive video-game market. Perhaps the same strategy is at hand with the Zune. After all, Microsoft certainly has the money and power to support the Zune and help it grow, both in market share and in technology.

So what makes the Zune so special in this crowded marketplace? Several features make it stand out significantly.

The first of these features is the oversize color screen. At 3 inches across, the screen is one of the largest available on a digital media player, making the viewing of video far more pleasurable than it is on a video iPod. In fact, the screen takes up nearly 70 percent of the Zune's front surface (**FIGURE 1.2**), but in today's visual world, that's an asset.

Figure 1.2
The screen on the Zune is huge (relatively speaking).

The second significant feature is the Zune's ability to transfer information through Wi-Fi. Each Zune has built-in wireless connectivity that lets it communicate with nearby Zunes and allows limited sharing of music and photos.

The Zune's feature list

Considering that the Zune practically appeared out of the ether, its feature list and capabilities are astounding. Remember, Microsoft hasn't had three or four generations of sales to hone its product to the market's every whim, so the fact that the Zune is this complete and versatile is a tribute to Microsoft's ability to produce any product when it puts its mind to it.

Check out the Zune's feature list:

- You can send music files (not all, but some) and photos from Zune to Zune via a wireless connection.

- The Zune software converts incompatible audio files to work with the device.

- Wi-Fi allows you to see nearby Zunes and what their owners are listening to.

- The Zune allows you to note tracks that you received via Wi-Fi transfers so that you can purchase them from Zune Marketplace.

- The Zune has limited podcast support.

- The Zune lets you create a playlist without connecting to the software.

- The built-in FM radio (**FIGURE 1.3**) can read Radio Data System information.

Figure 1.3
The Zune's FM radio is capable of receiving Radio Data System information.

- The Zune can play videos and show pictures or shuffle pictures in slideshows.

- Via the Zune tags feature, you can create a name and profile that nearby Zune users can see.

- The Zune's firmware is updatable, making its feature list expandable in the future.

 tip Although they're not sanctioned by Microsoft, quite a few hacks are already available to tweak the Zune. See Chapter 7 for more details.

The Zune's companions

In the introduction, I went over what comes in the box with your Zune, but I didn't talk about the various parts of the kit in detail. Although this discussion may seem like overkill, a few pieces of information are worth passing along.

Screen protector

The Zune comes packaged with a screen protector: a thin, peel-off piece of plastic with some messages printed on it. The large screen of the Zune is particularly susceptible to scratches, so using a screen protector is a good idea.

Screen protectors are available at electronics stores such as Best Buy, Circuit City, Future Shop (in Canada), and Radio Shack (The Source in Canada), as well as any number of Web sites; simply do a Web search for the words *screen protector*.

note

Many of these products are marketed as iPod screen protectors, but they work on anything—digital media players, cameras, mobile phones, and the like. The word *iPod* is in there only for marketing purposes.

Screen protectors are inexpensive, and they're well worth putting on your Zune the moment after you've taken it out of its case.

USB cable

The USB cable is a fairly standard connector, and straight out of the box, it's the only method for getting music onto your device—not to mention the only way you can charge it. Technically speaking, however, if you have a compatible USB power source, you can plug the Zune into it and successfully charge the device. You can purchase a power source as a standard wall jack with a USB connector that supplies standard USB power. You can also buy an external power charger and a car charger.

The beauty of USB is that it's hot-swappable, meaning that you can connect or disconnect the cable from your computer without fear of harming either one of them (in Windows 2000, XP, and Vista).

Although the Zune can connect to a USB 1.1 connector, using a USB 2.0 connector is highly recommended, entirely because of the speed differences between the two standards. Indeed, the USB 1.1 port charges your Zune just like the USB 2.0 port, but if you're moving 2 GB of data, what takes 30 seconds on a USB 2.0 port (**FIGURE 1.4**) might take 20 minutes on a USB 1.1 port.

Figure 1.4
Most contemporary PCs have USB 2.0 ports right on their front panels.

The Zune end of the USB cable is a proprietary size and shape, so it's important not to lose it; if you do, your Zune cannot transfer media or be charged. This connector (**Figure 1.5**) is not unlike the iPod connector; it's slightly smaller and has clips that keep it in place, requiring you to squeeze its sides to release it from the Zune.

Figure 1.5
The Zune's connector is proprietary, if somewhat familiar.

Headphones

The Zune's headphones are among the device's strong points. They aren't special stylistically, and their black cables don't particularly stand out, but they do produce excellent sound for their size.

They also have a convenience feature that I really appreciate: The stems of the headphones, just below the earbuds, are magnetic on both sides (**Figure 1.6**), which allows the two buds to snap together when not in use. This simple feature is actually a godsend when it comes to keeping the headphones from getting hopelessly tangled. It's a stroke of brilliance, and it wouldn't surprise me if everyone ended up using a similar strategy.

Figure 1.6
The magnetic earbuds make the Zune's headphones easier to manage when stored.

The headphones come with *socks*: those little spongy covers for the earbuds that make the buds sit tighter in your ear and add a small level of comfort to the experience.

Glove

The Zune comes with a small, soft, and stylish carrying case—the *glove* (**Figure 1.7**). Presumably, you'll use it only for storage, because when the Zune is in the glove, you can't see the controls or the screen.

Figure 1.7
The soft carrying case fits like a glove—perhaps a little too well.

The glove is a nice touch for storing the device, but it is a tight fit, so if you are trying to get the Zune out of the glove in cold weather, the chances of your dropping both items seem reasonable.

I suggest using the glove for storage at home or during light travel, not as a practical protector. A third-party carrying case probably is a superior option.

Software and instructions

The instructions for the Zune are nearly nonexistent (hey, that's why you have this book), but the startup disc is absolutely critical. Be sure not to lose that CD, because any time you want to reinstall the software (**Figure 1.8**), having the CD makes the job a heck of a lot easier.

Figure 1.8
The Zune startup CD contains only the Zune software.

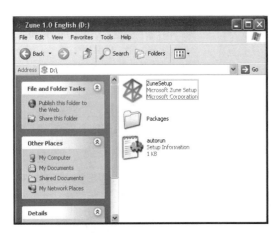

The startup CD's installation software includes an integrated browser/Zune controller (**Figure 1.9**) that connects to the Internet to obtain the latest help information and software/firmware updates for your Zune.

Figure 1.9
Once installed, the Zune software functions as a front end that uses the Internet extensively.

Zune Specifications

For those of you who like to know the nitty-gritty, down-and-dirty information about your consumer-electronics products, this section lists all the Zune's specifications, from size and weight right down to the battery and microprocessor that run it.

- Dimensions: 4.4 x 2.4 x 0.58 inches (11.2 x 6.1 x 1.4 centimeters)

- Weight: 5.6 ounces (158.9 grams)

- Wi-Fi: 802.11b/g standard

- Radio: FM receiver, Silicon Labs Si4701 radio tuner

- Hard drive: 30 GB, 1.8-inch Toshiba

- Screen type: 3-inch QVGA (Quarter Video Graphics Array) LCD (liquid crystal diode)

- Screen resolution: 320 x 240 pixels

- Formats supported: AAC, JPEG, WMV, WMA, MP3

- Battery life: up to 14 hours for music; up to 4 hours for video

- Battery: lithium-ion, 3.7 volts/800 mA

- Charge time: ≈3 hours (≈2 hours to 90 percent charge)

- USB: USB 2.0, Phillips

- Flash: 2 MB NOR flash, 3.3 volts

- CPU: Freescale i.MX31L processor

- RAM: 64 MB SDR DRAM at 133 MHz/90 mA

- Audio: stereo CODEC with speaker driver

- Audio power output: 0.9 watt

2

Interface and Function

Arguably, what set the iPod apart from its contemporaries and gave it a market edge is its easy-to-use menu system. A user can manage thousands of songs with just one digit (usually, a thumb), making it possible to find a specific song in a sea of music. Microsoft's challenge was to come up with a system for the Zune that's just as easy to use, or perhaps even easier than other players' systems, letting users maneuver through both music and visual content without pulling their hair out. Fortunately, Microsoft succeeded.

This chapter shows you how to manage your Zune and get full functionality out of it. The device has a lot to offer, but without diving deep into its inner workings, you might not know what's there for the taking.

The Face of Zune

First off, you'll want to get to know the Zune's controls (**Figure 2.1**). The Zune's largest feature is its 3-inch screen, occupying the top 70 percent of the unit. Below the screen is the circular control pad, a four-point input device that has click inputs at the compass points (top, bottom, left, and right).

Figure 2.1
A diagram of the Zune's controls.

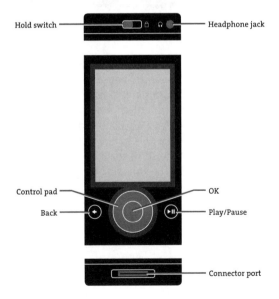

Hold switch

Headphone jack

Control pad

OK

Back

Play/Pause

Connector port

Inside the control pad is a single circular button that acts as the "select" button—officially, the OK button. Left of the control pad is the Back button, which takes you back one menu level each time it's pressed. Finally, to the right of the control pad is the Play/Pause button, which is used for the obvious reasons as well as for turning the Zune on and off.

Play/Pause button

The Play/Pause button is responsible for playing and pausing content, whether it's music, a video, or a photo slideshow. This button works as a play/pause toggle no matter what medium your Zune is working in, so feel free to use it as a control that you can rely on to stop the world when you want to get off for a second or two (like when you want to place your order at Starbucks, and you have to pause the music so you can hear the barista).

 If you're playing a picture slideshow along with some music, pressing the Play/Pause button pauses both the music and the slideshow, resuming them both when it's pressed a second time.

The other function of the Play/Pause button is its ability to turn the Zune off. If you want to shut the Zune down, press the button for 3 seconds, and the Zune turns itself off, saving valuable power.

The Play/Pause button is the only button that turns the Zune off, so don't get yourself caught spiraling through menus trying to use another button to shut 'er down.

tip Although Play/Pause is the only button that can shut the Zune down, you can use any of the buttons on the front of the Zune to turn it on. Indeed, it doesn't matter which front button you use; barring a dead battery, the Zune comes to life at a single touch.

Back button

The Back button does just what its name suggests: takes you back one menu level every time you press it. Therefore, no matter where you are in the Zune's menu structure, you can press Back to get back to the main menu (eventually).

This button takes you back through menus despite the music that's playing through the headphones (or speakers). In other words, simply navigating out of the music screen or radio screen back to the main menu (or any of the other menus) does not stop the music or radio program you are listening to. This is a nice feature that allows you to set up a slideshow while continuing to listen to the content you crave.

Control pad

At first glance, the control pad looks like it might be a scroll wheel à la the one on the iPod, but it has much more in common with the control pad on an Xbox controller than with an iPod's scroll wheel.

The control pad has four buttons on it, one at each of the compass points or "sides" of the circle, these being north, south, east, and west, otherwise known as up, down, right, and left. The use of these buttons depends entirely on what you're looking at onscreen. For the main menu, only the up and down controls serve any function, but in the Twist (the menu that runs horizontally on the top of some screens), the control pad's side buttons come into play.

OK button

The OK button is the one right smack-dab in the middle of the control pad. This button is what you press when you want to select whatever is highlighted onscreen. If the word *Play* is highlighted, for example, you can press OK to play the content, but you could press the Play/Pause button instead if you wanted.

More often than not, you'll use the OK button to select what you want in specific menus.

Hold switch

On the top of the Zune is a small toggle switch that slides toward an image of a lock or away from that same image. If the slider is close to the lock, the controls on the front of the Zune are locked out, making it impossible to use them to enter commands to the Zune. If the slider is farther from the lock sign, the controls are open and can be used.

This feature is surprisingly useful if you like to put the Zune in your pocket or wear it on a belt, and you bump into things a lot. By locking out the controls, you can guarantee that your music won't be interrupted or the volume drastically changed midsong. It's also important to lock the controls when the Zune isn't in use to ensure that it doesn't start playing something if the Play/Pause button is bumped, eventually draining the battery.

Headphone jack

How else can I put this? This is where you plug in your headphones. You can use the included headphones, and of course you can use others, such as the Bose Quiet Comfort noise-reduction headphones (a personal favorite).

Either way, be sure that the headphone plug is inserted firmly into the receptacle, because it is possible to get sound out of the headphones if the plug isn't seated properly. In this case, the sound is terrible but still in stereo, so you might not notice immediately that something isn't right.

Connector port

This port serves all purposes for the Zune: It connects the Zune to accessories, to your PC, to the car's 12-volt DC system for charging, and to the AC wall outlet in your home for charging. It probably is going to end up being the connecting point for a bevy of accessories that I haven't yet imagined, but suffice it to say that this little port on the bottom of the Zune is important. Don't allow your kids to stick their bubble gum (prechewed) in it for fun.

Negotiating the Menus

The Zune has a sizable set of menus, but considering what the device is capable of and all the data it can hold, the menu system is surprisingly simple, intuitive, and easy to use. That said, a few wrinkles are worth noting for novice users, so here goes.

The main menu (**Figure 2.2**) lists the six main areas your Zune manages: Music, Videos, Pictures, Radio, Community, and Settings. The following sections tell you what you can do in these areas.

Figure 2.2
The main menu.

The Twist

The Twist is the horizontal menu that slides across the top of the screen in some menus, including Music, Videos, and Pictures (but not limited to these). This menu is controlled by the side (left and right, or east and west) buttons on the control pad, thereby allowing you to move through two menus on the same screen. In other words, the vertical menu—perhaps a list of songs—is controlled by the up and down buttons of the control pad, and the left and right buttons control the Twist (or horizontal) menu at the top of the screen (**Figure 2.3**).

Figure 2.3
The Twist runs along the top of the screen.

lbums ‹ **artists** › playlists songs

Elton John
Fatboy Slim
Gilberto and Jobim
Harry Belafonte
Joey Aitruda
Kanda Bongo Man
Ludwig van Beethoven, composer
Marc Seales, composer. New Stor
Mel Tormé
New Stories

The Twist usually contains major categories such as Songs, Genres, Albums, and Artists in the case of music. Pressing the buttons moves you through the Twist quickly and efficiently. It's a great way to navigate two vectors of menus almost simultaneously. Certainly, the Twist allows you to see the headings in two discrete menus at the same time, and that in itself is quite handy indeed.

Music

Selecting the Music menu takes you to a dual-menu screen that has a Twist horizontally at the top and a menu that runs down the length of the screen. These two menus allow you to get to any piece of music on your Zune quickly and efficiently; they also allow you to make quick decisions and set up shuffling with ease.

The Music Twist contains these options:

- **Genres.** This option breaks the music down by genre: Classical, Latin, Rock, Jazz, Electronic, and so on.

- **Albums.** This option breaks down your entire music collection by album (**Figure 2.4**), with the album covers appearing in the vertical menu (along with the names of the albums). Whether you have one song from an album or the entire contents, the album cover still appears in this screen.

Figure 2.4
The Albums category gives you actual album covers to view along with text information about the artist(s).

nres ‹ **albums** › artists playlists

▶ shuffle all

Beethoven's Symphony No.
Seattle Symphony Orchestra

The Bethlehem Years
Mel Tormé

Carmina Angelica: The Conc
Various Artists

The Greatest Hits - Why Try
Fatboy Slim

Honky Chateau (Remastered
Elton John

Margarita Mix
Various Artists

- **Artists.** This option simply lists, in alphabetical order, all the artists represented on your Zune.

- **Playlists.** This option shows every playlist that you've created, either on the Zune or in the Zune software.

- **Songs.** The Songs option lists each and every song on your Zune (again, in alphabetical order), which can be a long list if you have thousands of songs on your device.

When you're scrolling through the list of songs, the Zune displays the appropriate letter of the alphabet on the right side of the screen (**Figure 2.5**) so that you can see just where you are in the list while the song titles whiz by. This is an amazingly handy feature that makes it much easier to sort through hundreds or thousands of titles.

Figure 2.5
Large white letters appear on the right side of the screen when you are scrolling through long song lists to let you know where you are in your scroll.

Videos

Videos are displayed vertically and can be selected with the control pad. To play a video, simply select the video in the menu and press the OK or Play/ Pause button.

Pictures

The Pictures screen lists all the pictures on the Zune (**Figure 2.6**). The vertical menu shows either the pictures themselves (with thumbnails) or thumbnails of one picture in a group sorted by either date or folder.

Figure 2.6
The main Pictures screen on the Zune.

The Twist contains several options, including:

- **View by Folder.** This option allows you to look at pictures according to the folder they reside in.

- **View by Date.** This option allows you to sort pictures by their date—grouped by month, so if you took 2,000 pictures in June 2006, there'll be 2,000 pictures in that folder.

When you select a specific month or group of pictures, the pictures in that group are displayed in a large thumbnail grid on the Zune screen, as shown in **FIGURE 2.7.** You can select the photo you want to look at, or you can use the control pad to move along the Twist, which now moves between folders or months to show you pictures from each group. At the top of the screen is a Play Slideshow button that plays a slideshow of the pictures in that particular group, if you so desire.

Figure 2.7
When you select an individual folder, the pictures appear in a large grid onscreen.

Using a Picture As Your Background

If you want to use a particular picture as the main background for your Zune, just press the OK button while you are viewing that picture and then choose Apply As Background from the menu. Voilà—the picture is the background/backdrop in every Zune screen (**FIGURE 2.8**).

Figure 2.8
Use any picture in your library as a background for the Zune.

Radio

Selecting the Radio menu immediately takes you to an FM radio band (**Figure 2.9**), from which you can select any FM station in the area. Use the control pad's left and right buttons to tune in the station you want to hear; then listen away.

Figure 2.9
The main Radio screen looks like an FM tuner— and what do you know? It is one.

Pressing the OK button on a station takes you to the presets screen (**Figure 2.10**), where you can set the station as a preset or remove it from the presets list.

Figure 2.10
The presets screen.

The Play/Pause button acts like a toggle button when the radio is playing, turning the speaker/headphone output on and off. The up/down controls on the control pad control the volume in the Radio screen, and as a bonus, you can alter the volume control while the speaker/headphone jack is turned off. It can be useful to keep these controls separate, and Microsoft has left them that way so that the Play/Pause button and the volume control do not overlap.

Community

The Community screen is the interpersonal part of the Zune's personality, showing you any nearby Zune users and the information they choose to let you see (**Figure 2.11**).

Figure 2.11
The Me option shows just what other Zune users can see on your Zune.

The Twist in this screen has three options:

- **Nearby.** This screen shows me the active Zune users who are close enough to communicate with.

- **Me.** This screen shows nearby Zune users your Zune tag (the name you gave your Zune), as well as the music or radio station you are listening to or the video you are watching.

- **Inbox.** This screen stores any pictures or music that have been sent to you from other Zunes via the Wi-Fi connection all Zunes employ. (Microsoft has called the act of wirelessly sending a file from one Zune to another *squirting*. So you might ask, "Hey, can you squirt me that song?")

When you're using the Zune's Wi-Fi communication features, the Community screen is quite simply the most important part of your Zune. From this screen, you can see who's around you, see what they're listening to or watching, and even offer to send them some music you think they may like. This could be the ultimate pickup device.

Settings

The Settings screen allows you to tweak your Zune in several ways, setting up the device's parameters just the way you like. Following are the Settings options and what you can do with them:

- **Wireless.** This option is a simple on/off toggle. In other words, if you don't want others to see you through your Zune, and you don't want to see others, set Wireless to off. If you are in a communicative mood, turn it to on.

The only catch to having Wireless turned on all the time is that it eats up your battery slightly faster, but this works out to about 10 percent faster (perhaps a smidgen more), which usually is worth it for most community-conscious folk.

- **Music.** There are three Music options in the Settings screen (**Figure 2.12**). Shuffle and Repeat are both on/off toggles and are self explanatory, but the third option, Equalizer, has a little more to it, because it tailors sound specifically for different styles of music. (Obviously, rock and roll does not require the same settings as a Chopin piano concerto.) The equalizer has eight distinct settings: acoustic, classical, electronica, hip-hop, jazz, pop, rock, and none. Check all of them out, because they definitely affect the sound of your music.

Figure 2.12
The Music settings.

tip If you switch headphones—moving from earbuds to noise-canceling headphones, for example—I recommend that you revisit your EQ settings. A new pair of headphones can make a huge difference.

- **Pictures.** The Pictures settings pertain specifically to the slideshow feature. The two options are Shuffle (on/off) and Transitions. When Shuffle is turned on, the Zune shuffles randomly among the pictures you are using in the slideshow; when Shuffle is off, the pictures are shown in order, from first to last. The Transitions option affects only the time between pictures in the slideshow. You can choose a setting of 3, 5, 7, 10, 15, or 30 seconds.

- **Display.** You can set four options in the Display screen (**Figure 2.13**). The first is Backlight, which regulates how long the screen remains illuminated after you last touched a button.

Figure 2.13
The Display screen allows you to manage (among other things) backlighting, brightness, and TV out.

display

themes
backlight: 15 seconds
brightness: high
tv out: off
tv system: NTSC

You can set the backlight in six ways: 1 second, 5 seconds, 15 seconds, 30 seconds, 1 minute, and always on. The main reason to alter these settings is to conserve battery power, because the backlight is one of the most "expensive" power users in the Zune.

The next two options are Brightness (high/medium/low) and TV Out (on/off). If you plan on running video or pictures to your television (you need a special cable to do this), TV Out must be set to the on position.

The last option is an NTSC/PAL toggle, but that's important only if you plan on traveling to Europe to show off your Zune.

- **Sounds.** This option can be set simply to on or off. Depending on this setting, button presses either produce sounds through the headphones/speakers, or they don't. Some people like to have the feedback; others are annoyed by it.

- **Radio.** The three Radio settings are North America, Europe, and Japan. Because these three countries use slightly different systems, you need to alter this setting if you travel to a different region. If you're reading this book, you are likely in North America, which is the default setting.

- **Online Status.** This option toggles between Basic and Detailed. Basic shows other Zune users only basic information about you, whereas Detailed shows them everything available, including what song you're listening to. It's essentially a privacy switch that's slightly less powerful than the Wireless on/off switch.

- **About.** This option takes you to a page with three choices: Zune, Storage, and Legal. Zune is a simple legal page with the Zune's firmware and software versions displayed, and the Legal page is just legal disclaimers. Storage, however, tells you how many songs, pictures, and videos you have stored on your device, as well as the space they take up on the Zune's hard drive (**Figure 2.14**).

Figure 2.14
The Storage screen is useful for finding out just how many media files you have on your Zune. It also shows you how much space is available on the Zune's hard drive.

storage
20 songs
446 pictures
1 video

0.33 GB used
27.43 GB free

3

Zune Software

The Zune is a wonder of modern technology and capable of doing fantastic things all on its own, but no matter how impressive the Zune appears when you're looking at it in your buddy's hand, the fact is that it requires a strong foundation. Someone (the source of this quote is unknown) once said, "Behind every great man is a great woman." In the case of the Zune, a great piece of software behind the Zune helps it rise to lofty levels in the realm of digital media players.

This chapter looks at the Zune software, what it can do, and how best to use it.

The Basics

This section examines the fundamentals of the Zune software, from installation to basic navigation to the various options and controls available to you. Much of this information is self-evident, but because the software does not come with an instruction manual (at least, not a printed manual), I can show you several things that you might not have been aware of otherwise.

Installation

Installing the Zune software is a breeze; just put the startup disc in your CD/DVD drive and let the autoplay function take over. You do not need to have the Zune attached to your PC at this point, but if you do, you won't damage it.

Following are a few of the steps that occur during installation.

 All the instructions in this section assume that you click the Next button when you finish each screen.

1. Put the Zune disc in your computer's CD/DVD drive.

    You see the Zune logo followed by the screen shown in **Figure 3.1.**

2. Follow the instructions to start the installation process.

    As the process moves along, the software shows you how far you have gone (as a percentage of the total), as well as some nifty pictures (**Figure 3.2**).

Figure 3.1
The first Zune Setup dialog box welcomes you to "the social" before installation begins.

Figure 3.2
Something to watch while you wait.

3. When the software is fully installed, restart your PC.

The software displays a screen with a Restart button to help you do that (**FIGURE 3.3**).

Figure 3.3
Click Restart to complete the installation.

Zune setup

Now that the Zune software is set up, you need to set a few parameters for the Zune itself. Connect the Zune to your computer and then follow the onscreen instructions:

1. In the Relocating? screen, specify whether you want to connect as a guest or to sync with the library (**FIGURE 3.4**).

Figure 3.4
Go with the guest option if you're not ready to lose the preinstalled content.

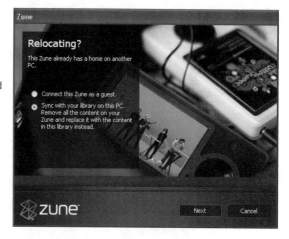

If you choose the sync option, the content that came with your Zune will be erased, so if you want to keep this content for a while, you need to connect as a guest.

Guest Sign-In

Whenever you connect a Zune, you get the option to synchronize the Zune with the library or sign in as a guest. If you choose the guest option, the Zune doesn't synchronize with your computer. This method is the one to use if you don't want the content on the Zune to be erased when you sync, or if you're at a friend's house and don't want to destroy what's on your Zune.

2. In the next screen, enter a name for your Zune (**Figure 3.5**).

Figure 3.5
Give your Zune the name that other people are going to see.

3. Indicate whether you want to sync videos and pictures between your Zune and the Zune software library (**Figure 3.6**).

Figure 3.6
Even if you don't choose to sync videos or pictures, your music will always synchronize, because the Zune syncs music automatically by default.

Manual Synchronization

If you want to have your Zune sync manually, connect your Zune to your PC; then, in the Navigation pane, right-click the device (the name of your Zune) and choose Set up Sync from the contextual menu. In the dialog box that appears, you'll see a check box labeled Sync This Device Automatically. If you check the box, the Zune always syncs upon connection; if you don't check it, you must synchronize the Zune manually every time.

4. Choose your library settings (**Figure 3.7**).

Usually, it's best to select the Express method, which is fine for most users.

Figure 3.7
Microsoft recommends that you pick Express, and so do I.

If you choose Custom, you see the Options dialog box (covered later in this chapter), which lets you make the Zune software the default player for various types of files (**Figure 3.8**). When you finish making choices in this dialog box, click OK to return to the Zune software, and go on to step 5.

Figure 3.8
You can set the software so that certain types of files trigger the Zune software by default.

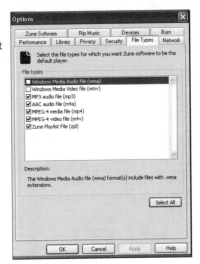

5. Decide whether you want to stream content to an Xbox 360 (**Figure 3.9**).

If you have an Xbox 360, you may as well choose Yes unless there's some reason why you don't want content on your gaming machine. (Perhaps you don't want another Xbox user to see some of your pictures or videos.)

Figure 3.9
Go ahead and stream to your Xbox if you've got one.

Zune account

The last part of the installation process is creating a Zune account, which effectively is part of your Windows Live ID. If you don't already have a Windows Live ID (many people do from using other Microsoft services), you can create one at this point.

1. First, create your Zune tag (**Figure 3.10**), which is the name that others will see when they view your Zune via Wi-Fi.

Figure 3.10
Your tag is your electronic name badge in the Zune community; it's the moniker by which you are identified.

2. Next, enter your Windows Live ID or, if you don't have one, create a new ID (**Figure 3.11**).

Figure 3.11
If you have an MSN or Hotmail account, you may already have this ID.

3. Finally, enter your address and other key information (**Figure 3.12**).

Figure 3.12
Fill out your personal info, and you're done.

Voilà—your account is set up (**FIGURE 3.13**). Now you can enjoy your Zune and the software that came with it.

Figure 3.13
You're ready to roll.

Navigation

The Zune software's main window is fairly straight-forward, but a few features may be a bit of a mystery, because they appear only as icons. **Figure 3.14** identifies each area and each menu item for you.

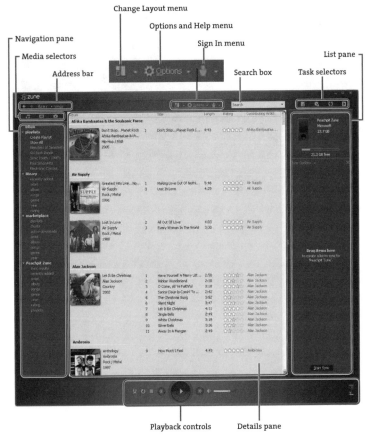

Change Layout menu

Options and Help menu

Sign In menu

Navigation pane

Media selectors

List pane

Address bar

Search box

Task selectors

Playback controls

Details pane

Figure 3.14 The Zune software main window.

Options, Controls, and Functions

This section looks at the various areas of the Zune software and explains its functions.

Navigation pane

The Navigation pane (**FIGURE 3.15**) is the area on the left side of the Zune software's main window. Click the links in this pane to go wherever you want to go, whether it's the Zune Marketplace main page or the album list in your personal Zune library.

The following sections discuss the areas you can access from this pane.

Marketplace

Clicking the main Marketplace link in the Navigation pane takes you to the main page of Zune Marketplace. If you click any of the categories below it instead—say, Artist, Charts, or Playlists—you immediately go to that area within the Marketplace. The results of your clicks are displayed in the Details pane in the middle of the window.

Figure 3.15
The Navigation pane.

You can choose any of the following Marketplace categories:

- Playlists displays the Playlists area of Zune Marketplace.

- Charts shows you the charts so that you can see what's tops in sales and popularity.

- Active Downloads shows you the downloads that are currently queued or downloading (**Figure 3.16**).

- Artist organizes by artist.

- Album organizes by album.

- Songs lists content by song.

- Genre breaks down music for sale by genre.

- Year breaks down music by the year it was created/released.

Figure 3.16
Active downloads are displayed in the Details pane.

Library

The Library section of the Navigation pane represents the actual files on your computer's hard drive (in the My Documents > My Music > Zune folder). The Library categories help you organize by particular methods, which are:

- Recently Added shows the content most recently added to your library.

- Artist organizes by artist.

- Album organizes by album.

- Songs lists content by song.

- Genre breaks down music for sale by genre.

- Year breaks down music by the year it was created/released.

- Rating organizes content by your rating (1 to 5 stars).

Playlists

The Playlists category simply lists all the playlists you've created (**Figure 3.17**). If you have a huge number of playlists, however, you'll see only the top six or seven of them and a Show All button; to display all your playlists, click Show All.

Figure 3.17
The first six or seven playlists are combined here.

Inbox

The inbox is the place where items you've flagged are placed. (See Chapter 5 for the how-to on flagging.) If you flag a piece of music or a video, it appears in the inbox as an opportunity for you to erase it, contemplate it, download it, or purchase it.

The content's status is listed on the right side of the Details pane (**Figure 3.18**). If you want to purchase or download an item, simply click the Purchase or Download link; it's that simple.

Figure 3.18
The inbox shows you flagged items and their status.

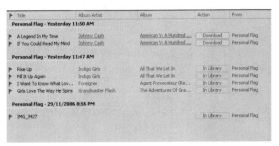

List pane

The List pane is the area on the right side of the screen. The information you see in this pane depends on the four buttons at the top of the pane: Playlist, Burn Files to Disc, Synchronize, or Now Playing (**Figure 3.19**).

Figure 3.19
These four buttons control the display in the List pane.

Playlist   Burn Files to Disc   Synchronize

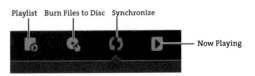

Now Playing

Create and edit playlists

Click the Playlist button (refer to Figure 3.19) to create and edit complex playlists in the Zune software. All you have to do is drag the album, the artist, or individual songs to the area of the List pane that says *Drag items here to create a playlist* (**FIGURE 3.20**).

Figure 3.20
Creating a playlist is as easy as dropping songs in the List pane.

The top of the List pane shows you how many items are in the playlist and how many minutes the playlist occupies (**FIGURE 3.21**). This is important, because standard audio CDs can hold about 80 minutes of music, so if you are planning on burning the playlist to an audio CD, you need to watch its size.

Figure 3.21
Keep an eye on the playlist's size.

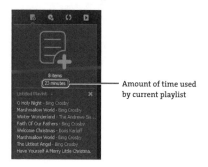

Amount of time used by current playlist

The drop-down menu at the top of the play-list (**Figure 3.22**) gives you access to a slew of commands, including these:

- Shuffle List Now shuffles the songs in the playlist, which is handy if you want a random spread to burn onto a CD.

- Sort sorts songs by the usual means (artist, songs, genre, album, release date, rating, and file name).

- Rename Playlist lets you change the playlist's name.

- Save Playlist As saves your handiwork.

- Create Playlist lets you start from scratch.

- Edit Playlist lets you change the content of a playlist.

Figure 3.22
A playlist's drop-down menu.

Burn files to CD

Click the Burn Files to Disc button (refer to Figure 3.19) to bring up the CD-burning display.

Before you begin the process, you need to choose between a data CD and an audio CD. An *audio CD* is the kind that plays in any audio CD or DVD player, whereas a *data CD* usually works only in a computer.

tip **Creating a data CD is useful if you want to back up a large number of songs.**

Make your choice from the Burn Options drop-down menu (**Figure 3.23**), which also lets you rename the disc and level the volume across all tracks on the CD.

Figure 3.23
You have plenty of options in the Burn Options menu.

To burn a disc, insert a blank CD into your computer's CD/DVD drive and drag your desired content to the section of the List pane that says *Drag items here to create a burn list*. Then click the Start Burn button at the bottom of the List pane.

Sync up

Click the Synchronize button (refer to Figure 3.19) to
see the Synchronize area (**Figure 3.24**), which asks
you to connect a Zune device. Then you can do a
general sync, which synchronizes your entire library
with the Zune, or a custom sync.

Figure 3.24
The Synchronize
area works
much like
the Playlist
area. The Sync
Options drop-
down menu lets
you customize
the process.

To do a general sync, simply connect the Zune and
then click the Start Sync button (unless you've set
up the Zune to synchronize automatically, in which
case the process starts by itself). If your Zune is set
to sync manually, and you want to synchronize only
certain files, drag them to the List pane and then
click the Start Sync button. That's it!

See what's playing

When you click the Now Playing button (refer to Figure 3.19), the List pane displays information on whatever you're looking at in the Navigation pane, so if you're looking at a particular album, that album is displayed.

Change Layout menu

The Change Layout menu contains three view options: Icon, Tile, and Details. Details view displays songs in the Details pane with as much information as possible (**Figure 3.25**).

Figure 3.25
Details view.

Tile view, however, provides a nice combination of
album covers and information (**Figure 3.26**), and Icon
view displays generic icons.

Figure 3.26
Tile view.

The last option in the Change Layout menu, Choose
Columns, displays a dialog box (**Figure 3.27**) that lets
you decide exactly what columns are displayed when
you view your songs in the Details pane. If you want
to remove the Length category and replace it with
Mood, for example, go right ahead.

Figure 3.27
The Choose Columns dialog box allows you to set up the columns (categories or classifications) in which your songs are displayed.

Options and Help menu

The Options and Help menu contains many settings that you can tweak (**Figure 3.28**). You can also use the Options dialog box (covered later in the chapter) to alter key aspects of the Zune software.

Figure 3.28
This menu lets you customize the Zune software.

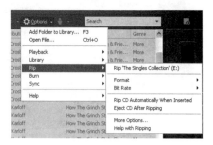

The following sections describe the main options in this menu.

Playback

The Playback options allow you to turn the visualizer on and off, as well as adjust the equalizer settings (**Figure 3.29**):

- Acoustic

- Classical

- Electronica

- Hip Hop

- Jazz

- Pop

- Rock

- Off

Figure 3.29
You can access the equalizer settings by choosing Options and Help > Playback > Equalizer.

The Help with Playback option is also available in the Help section (described later in this chapter), and More Options takes you to the Options dialog box.

Library

The Library options allow you to adjust the media-sharing settings for the Xbox 360 and for other computers connected to your network. Also, Find Info for All Albums sends the Zune software out on the Internet to look for more details on all the music in your library, from album art to the spelling of artists' names.

Rip

The Rip options let you rip the current CD in your CD/DVD drive, as well as set what format the music is ripped into (WMA or MP3) and the bit rate (quality level). For details on the process, see the "Ripping a CD" sidebar later in this chapter.

Burn

The Burn options allow you to burn playlists to audio or data CDs. You can also apply volume leveling across all tracks so that there are no drastic differences in volume between tracks on the newly created CD.

Sync

The options in this submenu are much like those in the Sync Options drop-down list, in that they allow you to find a connected Zune and synchronize it with the library on your PC.

Help

Choose the Help command to open the Help Center (**Figure 3.30**), which is a great asset and should be the first place you look when you're really stumped. The Help Center gives you information about nearly every aspect of using your Zune in easy-to-understand language.

Figure 3.30
The Zune Help Center is an outstanding reference.

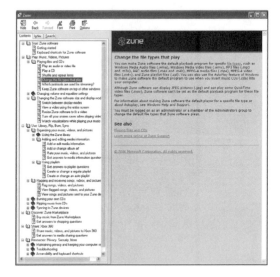

The Options Dialog Box

The Options dialog box (**FIGURE 3.31**) appears when you choose Options and Help > More Options. You can tweak all the nitty-gritty details of the Zune software on the following tabs:

- **Performance.** Set your Internet connection speed, network buffering, and video acceleration (used mostly with the visualizer).

- **Library.** Set the sharing privileges for your library, as well as automatic information updates for your music.

- **Privacy.** Indicate whether you want to send software usage data to Microsoft. The options on this tab also let you clear out caches on your computer that the Zune software uses.

- **Security.** Alter security levels within the Zune software.

continues on next page

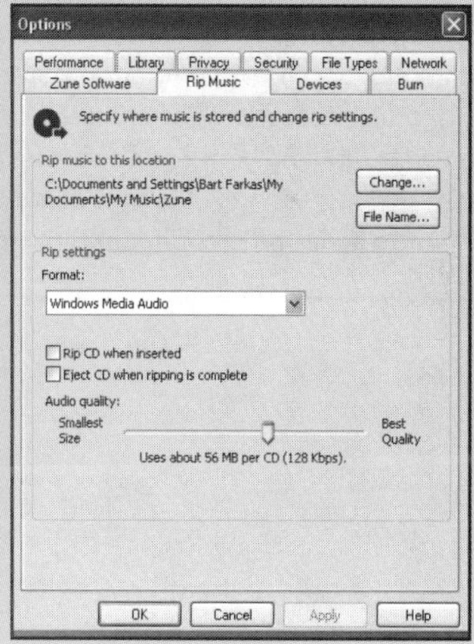

Figure 3.31
The Options
dialog box.

The Options Dialog Box *continued*

- **File Types.** Set which file types are linked to the Zune software.

- **Network.** Set the protocol for your network and configure it. (Most people never touch these settings.)

- **Zune Software.** Alter basic settings for the Zune software, such as Always on Top.

- **Rip Music.** Set the format of ripped music, its quality, and the location where the music is ripped.

- **Devices.** See which devices are available to the Zune software. You may have more than one Zune and/or multiple CD/DVD drives (because you can rip music from them).

- **Burn.** Set the burn speed, the quality of music conversion, and other aspects of burning.

 tip Setting automatic information updates for your music gives your library the proper album covers, artwork, song names, song length, artist information, and other details for your music collection. Sometimes, this information changes, so allowing your Zune software to check for and update newly ripped music is a great way to keep your library up to date and accurate (in terms of information).

Sign In menu

The Sign In menu (**Figure 3.32**) is where you log into your Zune/Windows Live account. It's also where you access the Account Management area to change such things as your password, billing information, and address, as well as to purchase Zune Passes and Microsoft Points.

Figure 3.32
The Sign In menu.

Ripping a CD

The process of ripping a CD to your Zune software library is very easy, but before you start, you probably should check the settings and make sure that they are to your liking.

With your Zune software open and running, follow these steps:

1. In the main software window, choose Options and Help > Rip > Format; then, from the Format submenu, choose Windows Media Audio, Windows Media Audio Lossless, or MP3 (**Figure 3.33**).

continues on next page

Figure 3.33
Pick the format you want to use.

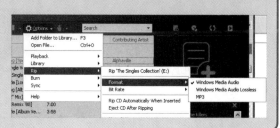

Ripping a CD *continued*

2. Choose Options and Help > Rip > Bit Rate, and select the bit rate at which you want to record the files (**Figure 3.34**).

Figure 3.34
Choose a bit rate.
Remember that
the higher the bit
rate, the higher
the sound quality
of the song.

3. Drop an audio CD into your CD/DVD drive.

The CD appears in the Details pane (**Figure 3.35**). After a quick Internet access, the Zune software displays the name, artist, time, and other details on each song (and usually the album cover as well).

Figure 3.35
You get a
preview
of the CD
you're about
to rip.

4. Click the Start Rip button at the bottom of the pane to start the rip.

You can see the songs being ripped to your library one at a time. The songs that have already been ripped are labeled Ripped to Library; an orange-to-pinky-red progress bar appears next to the song that is being ripped at the moment; and songs that have yet to be ripped are labeled Pending (**Figure 3.36**).

Figure 3.36
Follow the progress of the rip in this screen.

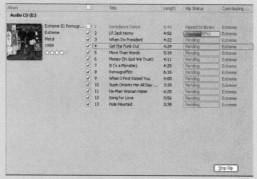

Also note the display at the bottom of the pane that says *Ripping: X tracks remaining* (**Figure 3.37**).

Figure 3.37
The Zune software lets you know how many more tracks are waiting to be ripped.

When all the tracks are ripped, that's it. They appear in your library.

4

Zune Marketplace

Digital media players like the Zune are fantastic devices with a great deal to offer, but without a standardized place to purchase music and other media content, the device can't compete with the market leaders. Not to worry, Zune owners: Microsoft has Zune Marketplace, which contains millions of songs for immediate download.

Zune Marketplace is a unique animal in that it uses a point system instead of actual cash (although points are essentially the same thing). It also offers a special Zune Pass that allows you to download nearly any music you want for use on your Zune, with the caveat that you cannot transfer or burn that music to a CD or a hard drive.

This chapter examines Zune Marketplace and takes you through the process of managing your account.

Setting Up an Account

To use Zune Marketplace, you need a Windows Live account. After you install your Zune software from the startup CD, you are given the option to enter a Windows Live ID (if you already have one) or create a new one (**Figure 4.1**).

Figure 4.1
You need to enter your Windows Live ID or create one.

Next, sign in to your Zune account with your Windows Live ID (**Figure 4.2**). In the sign-in screen, you have the option to let the software save your email address and password, save just your email address, or ask for both every time you log on.

Figure 4.2
Set up how your
sign-in is going
to be from here
on out.

In the following screen, you're asked to enter your
account information—such as name, address, and
date of birth—as well as a contact email address
(**Figure 4.3**).

Figure 4.3
Get ready to
sign your life
away.

Finally, you need to review and accept the terms of use and privacy statement.

That's it! The last screen congratulates you (by name) and tells you that you're signed up for Zune.

Now you have three choices: Go to Zune Marketplace, Buy Microsoft Points, and Get a Zune Pass subscription (**Figure 4.4**). Before you dive in, though, you should know about the Microsoft Points system and the ins and outs of the Zune Pass.

Figure 4.4
Zune
Marketplace
awaits.

Initiating Your Free Zune Pass

Before you go into Zune Marketplace to buy stuff and look around, you may as well find the card that came with your Zune (**FIGURE 4.5**). The back (the white side) of this card contains a 25-digit code that you enter in the Account Management area to claim a 14-day Zune Pass. This pass is 100 percent free—no strings attached. You don't even have to enter a credit card to activate this puppy, so it's well worth doing.

Figure 4.5
The 25-digit code on the back of this card is your ticket to a free Zune Pass.

note To activate your Zune Pass or purchase Microsoft Points—or to change your account information, for that matter—you need to be connected to the Internet.

To redeem the pass, click the head-and-torso icon at the top center of the Zune software window; then drag down to Account Management. You arrive at an Account Summary page with nine options (**Figure 4.6**):

- **Account Management.** Clicking this button takes you to the MSN Account Settings Web page at Microsoft. Here, you can manage many aspects of your MSN (or Windows Live ID) account, such as changing your email address, your password, or your address, and even access customer support.

- **Family Settings.** The Family Settings area gives parents a way to protect their children in Zune Marketplace by limiting access to certain kinds of content.

Figure 4.6
From this page, you can control the important (financial) matters of your account.

- **Change Password.** Just as the name suggests, this area is where you go to change your password.

- **Zune Pass.** Click this button to purchase a 1-month or 3-month pass.

- **Purchase Points.** This area is where you can use good old cash to buy Microsoft Points, which you use to purchase media in Zune Marketplace.

- **Redeem Prepaid Card.** When you click this button, you go to a screen where you can enter the code for your free 14-day Zune Pass or any prepaid card you may have acquired.

- **Rights Management.** This area keeps track of which computers you are using with your Zune. Currently, you can play your subscription music on three computers, but if you want to add another computer or delete one, this is the place to do it.

- **Restore Library.** This option allows you to restore your Zune quickly with all the music you have purchased through Zune Marketplace.

- **Incomplete Transactions.** Sometimes, due to a variety of problems, such as network or Internet difficulties, transactions end up incomplete. When this happens, you can go to this area to clear up the transactions one way or another.

Click the Redeem Prepaid Card button, enter your code in the boxes on the next screen (**FIGURE 4.7**), and then click Redeem. Your 14-day Zune Pass is activated for your pleasure. You can use this same method to redeem other prepaid cards you received as gifts or purchased elsewhere.

Figure 4.7
Enter your code here. (By the way, the code in this screen isn't the real thing.)

Dealing with Money Matters

Zune Marketplace runs on Microsoft Points and Zune Passes. These two commodities allow very different types of access to Zune Marketplace's wares, but they also interact to provide an overarching product.

Microsoft Points

You can purchase these points in the Account Management area of the Zune software and on Zune.net, after which they appear on your account and are subtracted accordingly as you buy items.

Microsoft Points are worth 1.25 cents each, or 80 points for every dollar. Points are sold in four categories (**Figure 4.8**):

- 400 for $5

- 1,200 for $15

- 2,000 for $25

- 4,000 for $50

Figure 4.8
You have four point-purchase options in this screen.

Most songs sell for 79 points, or 98.75 cents each. Albums usually cost in the neighborhood of 1,200 points, which is $15. Compared with other digital music stores, the prices are right on target.

The other interesting thing about Microsoft Points is that they can be used across the Zune Marketplace and Xbox platforms, giving you a single option for purchasing for both the Zune and the Xbox.

The Zune Pass

The Zune Pass is an innovative concept that allows the user partial access to more than 2 million tracks in Zune Marketplace for the relatively low cost of just $14.99 per month. You can purchase Zune Passes in 1-month or 3-month flavors, but the per-month cost is the same whichever option you choose, so you don't save money by buying more than one month at a time (**Figure 4.9**).

Figure 4.9
Choose between 1-month and 3-month Zune Passes.

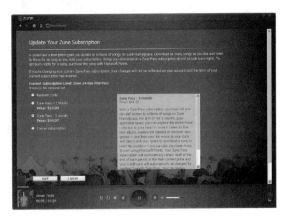

The bonus of the Zune Pass is that you can download most music in Zune Marketplace straight to your library and then place it on your Zune for immediate listening. It's best described as a "play before you pay" option that lets you listen to the music and keep it in your library as long as you have an active Zune Pass. It's like renting the music on a month-by-month basis instead of buying it. And there really is no limitation on listening to the music you download with the Zune Pass, because you can place the songs on your Zune device and play them as much as you want as long as your Zune Pass is active.

If the Zune Pass seems too good to be true—that is, full access to 2 million songs for $14.95 per month—don't worry, because there's no hidden small print. The bottom line is that you pay the $15 per month and get access to a whole lot of music.

There are a couple of small limitations, however, including the fact that not all the music in Zune Marketplace is available to Zune Pass holders. Generally speaking, though, music that is not available is relatively uncommon.

The other limitation is that the music you download to your Zune and your Zune software library via a Zune Pass cannot be burned onto a CD. If you try to burn this material to a CD, the dialog box shown in **FIGURE 4.10** gives you the option to buy the content (and then continue with your CD burn). This makes sense, because after a song is burned onto a CD, it essentially loses its copy protection and can be moved around with greater ease.

Figure 4.10
If you try to burn content obtained under a Zune Pass, you immediately get the option to cease what you're doing or buy the content and continue.

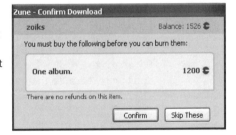

Zune - Confirm Download

zoiks   Balance: 1526 ₢

You must buy the following before you can burn them:

One album.   1200 ₢

There are no refunds on this item.

[Confirm]   [Skip These]

Navigating Zune Marketplace

To get to Zune Marketplace, just click the word *Marketplace* on the left side of the Zune software window (**Figure 4.11**). As long as you are connected to the Internet, the Zune Marketplace main screen appears in the central window, displaying featured artists, new releases, and playlists from various sources.

The main page is interactive, so mousing over specific album covers in the New Releases area brings that particular album to the forefront. This section explains the various areas of the main page.

Figure 4.11
Click the Marketplace link to go to Zune Marketplace's main page.

Main miniwindow

This large window takes up the top-left corner of Zune Marketplace's main page. Thumbnails for five main themes or albums keep rotating into the miniwindow as you view the main page. Click any of these thumbnails or the main miniwindow itself to see details on the album that's being promoted (**Figure 4.12**).

Figure 4.12
The largest miniwindow on the Zune Marketplace main page is a good starting point.

Featured Artists

The Featured Artists area in the bottom-right corner of the main page spotlights four artists at a time, and the top-right corner of the screen sometimes features artists in one or more of its four slots. Clicking a featured artist sends you not to the artist's latest album but to a page that displays that artist's entire slate of albums available in Zune Marketplace (**FIGURE 4.13**).

Figure 4.13
Click a featured artist to see all of that artist's albums at Zune Marketplace.

New Releases

The New Releases area is a list of albums, represented only by their covers. Mousing over each cover
gives you more specific information, and if you are
interested in getting a detailed look, click the orange
double right arrow next to the words *New Releases*.
You are taken to a page that displays new releases by
date or genre (your choice), as shown in **Figure 4.14**.

Figure 4.14
The New
Releases list can
be filtered by
week or genre.

Playlists

Playlists are interesting phenomena. If you are unfa-miliar with what a playlist is, allow me to educate you: Playlists are groups of songs that people like to compile and place on their digital music players and then play through sequentially or shuffle through randomly. They're highly personal, reflecting not only a person's musical taste but also some aspects of his or her personality. Celebrity playlists have become a recent craze, with journalists often asking "What's on your iPod?" during interviews with famous folk.

The Playlists area of Zune Marketplace contains already-assembled general playlists; celebrity play-lists; genre-specific playlists; and even "dig in" play-lists, which delve deeply into a single artist, genre, concept, or feeling (**FIGURE 4.15**). It's a fairly cool way to see what's out there musically, and it's a fantastic way to expose yourself to new and interesting music—or, for that matter, to old and forgotten music that still has the ability to send chills up or down your spine.

When you think about it, if you really love a certain artist—Brian Ferry, for example—and you see that he has submitted a playlist, you are likely to be very interested to see just what he likes to listen to and to check it out yourself. Playlists are a great idea that is likely to keep on rolling for years to come.

Figure 4.15
Playlists are a
great way to
get exposed
to new music.

Sampling Music

One great thing about Zune Marketplace is that you
can listen to each and every one of the millions of
available songs before you purchase or download
it. Well, OK, you can't listen to the songs all the way
through, but you can sample half a minute or so of
any song you want to purchase, which lets you get
a feel for what you're buying before you plop down
your hard-earned Microsoft Points on the barrelhead.

To listen to a song's sample, simply double-click the song in question, and the 30-second snippet plays for you (**FIGURE 4.16**). The controls at the bottom center of the window let you adjust the volume or terminate playback (by clicking the Pause button).

Figure 4.16
Sampling music is the way to go. After all, "try before you buy" is a proven paradigm in retail.

The one caveat to the 30-second-sample rule is this: If you are using a Zune Pass, you can listen to any song available for download in its entirety before you actually download it. When you think about it, that makes sense; why limit how long people can listen to a song if you are going to let them download it anyway?

Finding Music

With literally millions of songs in Zune Marketplace, you might think that finding the music you want would be a daunting task, but the powerful Search feature makes finding nearly any song or artist a snap. To begin with, the Search area, below the Marketplace heading on the left side of the Zune software window, lists several search options:

- Playlists
- Charts
- Active Downloads
- Artist

- Album
- Songs
- Genre
- Year

Being able to sort through songs via any one of these filters is very handy, but if you really want to narrow down a search, simply type a keyword in the search field and press the Enter key. In a matter of seconds, you have a list of artists, songs, and albums related to whatever you typed (**FIGURE 4.17**).

Figure 4.17
The search engine in Zune Marketplace is very powerful.

If you type **Safety Dance** in the search engine and press Enter, for example, you get 41 distinct hits on it. Usually, what ends up happening is that you find the song you want, plus ten or more covers of that same song, with a few live versions thrown in for fun.

Purchasing Albums or Songs

To purchase a song or album, first you need to get some Microsoft Points (covered earlier in this chapter) in your account; then you need only click the Buy button that appears to the right of any given song. Up in the album window, you can purchase the entire album (**Figure 4.18**) for a price that's usually between 800 and 1,200 points.

Figure 4.18
You can purchase an entire album by clicking one link.

After you click the Buy button, the process of downloading the songs begins automatically. You can see how the downloads are progressing by clicking the Active Downloads link on the left side of the window, below the Marketplace header (**Figure 4.19**).

Figure 4.19
The Active
Downloads
page shows you
the progress
of all of your
downloads.

If you are using a Zune Pass, many songs won't have
a Buy button next to them; instead , they'll have
a Download link. If you want to bypass the initial
download and simply purchase the song, right-click
the Download icon and choose Buy from the contextual menu (**Figure 4.20**). This choice purchases the
song and downloads it to your library automatically.

Figure 4.20
With a right-
click and a
menu selection,
you can buy
a song that's
otherwise
targeted for
a Zune Pass
download.

Using the Music

So now that you have all this music in your Zune software library, what are you going to do with it? First, you can listen to it on your PC, and if you have a fancy sound system attached to your computer, you can get some great enjoyment out of your music.

Alternatively, you can put all that music on your Zune for enjoyment on the go. With 30 GB of space on the Zune, there's plenty of room for thousands of songs that you can take on the road. Create specific playlists by dragging specific songs to the Playlist window and then naming the playlist. That's all there is to it!

If you want to create a music CD, you need only click the Burn icon and insert a blank CD. With a click of the album name, you can select an audio or a data CD. The difference between the two is that an audio CD plays in any standard CD or DVD player, whereas a data CD contains the actual MP3 files, which can be played only on devices that are capable of reading MP3s off CD-ROMs.

Making Connections

The Zune is a fine MP3 player and a fantastic video player, and the sound quality (to my ears) is up there with the best of them, but a few more aspects of the Zune are worth discussing. The Zune can connect to an Xbox 360 via a USB cable, for example, and stream music and video to the gaming device—but not to be outdone, the Zune software on your Windows PC also can stream music, video, and photographs to an Xbox 360 on the same network. When this suite of features works, it's impressive, to say the least.

This chapter looks at the Wi-Fi functionality of the Zune as well as its Xbox 360 connectivity and shows you how to get both features up and running.

Why Wi-Fi?

Wi-Fi is the standard term for an IEEE (or Institute of Electrical and Electronics Engineers) 801.11 wireless network connection. It started to take hold in the late 1990s, helped in part when Apple introduced a laptop with Wi-Fi in 1999.

Wi-Fi speeds have progressed and now can deliver as much as 54 Mbps through the ether. It's safe to say that Wi-Fi is an industry standard today; nearly every laptop has a wireless card embedded in it, and so do many desktop computers, from Macs to PCs.

note Wi-Fi is an awesome technology and extremely handy, but some limitations are worth noting. The most glaring limitation is that some popular flavors of Wi-Fi uses the spectrum around 2.4 GHz—frequencies similar to those used by many cordless telephones and micro-wave ovens. The result is that when you're using a phone or microwave, the network has a tendency to go down.

tip I used to have this very problem with my phones inter-fering with my wireless network. This was fairly frus-trating, because my computers had to go looking for a new network every time I got a phone call. Ultimately, I switched my 2.4 GHz phone to a 5.8 GHz model. Problem solved. It's usually not much of a headache, but if you have several appliances and other devices that use those frequencies, take note of them before setting up a network in the same frequency range.

The Zune and Wi-Fi

The Zune is equipped with a Wi-Fi card that both sends and receives information. This could be an extremely powerful feature, but the folks at Microsoft made the Zune's Wi-Fi respond only to other Zunes, which means that you can't use an Internet Wi-Fi hotspot to download new tunes to your Zune via Zune Marketplace.

For now, we must settle for what Wi-Fi actually does on the Zune—and even the most jaded of us must admit that it's still pretty darned cool.

Community Wi-Fi

The most-publicized communication feature of the Zune is its ability to set up an ad hoc Zune-to-Zune wireless connection and then share photos and music files over Wi-Fi with whomever happens to be standing nearby with another Zune: a friend, an acquaintance, or even a complete stranger.

To use the Zune in a community environment, first you have to decide whether you want it to broadcast detailed or basic information about you. To change this setting, choose Settings from the main menu and then choose Online Status to select the mode you want to project to others.

The only difference between the two modes is that Basic doesn't display what you're listening to and Detailed (**FIGURE 5.1**) shows everyone just what you have in your ears.

Figure 5.1
Choosing between Detailed and Basic modes in the Online Status section of the Settings menu.

I suspect that if you decide to engage in a marathon play of Carpenters tunes, you may be inclined to keep the setting closer to the Basic side. The real fun of the Zune, however, is seeing what others are listening to, so I like to take a chance (even if I'm listening to ABBA) and let it all hang out with Detailed mode active.

The rules of sharing music

One of the big selling points of the Zune is the "share music with friends or strangers via Wi-Fi" angle. Including Wi-Fi in the Zune is a great idea, but it has some limitations.

The rules for sharing a file or song on the Zune are as follows:

- You can send as many songs to other Zune owners as you want and receive as many songs as you want.

- Some songs from Zune Marketplace do not have send rights and, therefore, cannot be shared.

- Songs you receive from other Zune members are called *sample songs*. You can play sample songs 3 times before they expire—but sample songs expire automatically after 3 days whether they've been played or not.

 You can see how many plays and how much time you have left on a sample song by selecting it and then choosing Details.

- When you synchronize your Zune with your PC, information about the sample songs you've received is placed in the inbox in the Zune software, allowing you to find and purchase them later (if you so desire).

- When songs, videos, or pictures are sent to your Zune, they appear in the inbox in the Community section of the main menu.

Practical sharing points

Some members of the media have criticized Microsoft's sharing rules for the Zune device, but when you look objectively at the rules, they don't impinge much at all, considering that copying music between people is illegal. Yes, a song that's shared between two people can be played only 3 times, and yes, it is locked out after 3 days (regardless of how many times you listened to it), but 3 listens should be enough to decide whether you want a song or not.

The major downside to the sharing process is that music you've made yourself or music that's in the public domain (under a Creative Commons license, for example) is still subject to the 3-play/3-day rule. I hope that this restriction can be fixed down the road, but as things stand right now, even a song that you wrote and recorded yourself ends up being locked out.

 Microsoft says it's going to build up the Zune's wireless capabilities in upcoming releases of the player and software, so I hope it fine-tunes this part of sharing.

If you like it, flag it!

If someone sends you a song, you can either listen to it 3 times or keep it on your Zune for 3 days before it goes away forever. If, however, you flag the song with the Zune, you can pull it up and purchase it later, or download it with a Zune Pass.

To put a flag on a song:

1. Play the song on your Zune (**Figure 5.2**).

Figure 5.2
Start by playing
the song you
want to flag.

2. Press the OK button (the button in the middle
    of the control pad) to display the play options
    (**Figure 5.3**).

Figure 5.3
Scroll down to
find the Flag
option.

3. Choose Flag from the menu, and then press the OK button again (**FIGURE 5.4**).

Figure 5.4
Your song is flagged.

4. Synchronize the Zune with your PC (and Zune software) to place the song in your inbox in the Zune software window (**FIGURE 5.5**).

Figure 5.5
The Zune software displays (what else?) a flag icon next to flagged songs in your inbox.

Flagging a song is a way of ensuring that you won't lose the identity of that song when the trial period expires. If you receive ten songs from another Zune user, and you listen to all ten, but you like only two of them enough to play them again, take the time to flag those two songs. If they're available in Zune Marketplace, you'll see Download links in your inbox

(**Figure 5.6**); then you can purchase those songs or add them to your library via a Zune Pass (assuming that the songs are available to Zune Pass holders).

Figure 5.6
Flagged songs in Zune Marketplace appear in your inbox all ready to go.

If a flagged song isn't available in Zune Marketplace, the Zune software can go out on the World Wide Web to search for it.

The Zune and the Xbox 360

If you are enough of a Microsoft aficionado that you also own an Xbox 360, you're in luck, because you can share music from the Zune software on your PC via network connections as well as directly from your Zune to the Xbox via a USB cable.

Although this isn't likely to be something that all Zune users are going to do, there are some nice benefits to being able to stream music to the Xbox. After all, if you can listen to your own music while you play a game, why not do it?

Streaming from your PC to the Xbox 360

The Zune software can stream content directly to your Xbox 360 via a shared network. As long as your PC and your Xbox are on the same network (or are connected through a router), you can "see" the Xbox from your computer and send information to it from your Zune software—which is de facto your Zune device, because the content on your PC is the same as that on your Zune, barring any recently shared music or other media files.

Several pieces have to fall into place for you to get files streaming to your Xbox, the first of which is ensuring that your Zune software is configured to stream in that direction.

Setting up the PC

When you install the Zune software, you are given the option to stream to the Xbox 360 (**Figure 5.7**), so if you want to do that, be sure to check the boxes that allow sharing.

Figure 5.7
When you first set up your Zune software, you get the option to allow streaming to an Xbox 360.

If you didn't choose that option during installation, not to worry. Here's how to get your Zune software streaming to your 360:

 These directions assume that your Xbox 360 and your Windows PC (with the Zune software installed on it) are connected to a shared network.

1. If you don't already have it, install Windows Media Player 11 on your PC (**Figure 5.8**).

   You can get Media Player for free (go to http://www.microsoft.com/windows/windowsmedia/default.mspx).

Figure 5.8
Installing
Windows Media
Player 11.

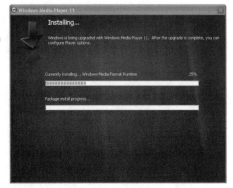

2. After installation, launch Media Player and choose Tools > Options (**Figure 5.9**) to open the Options dialog box.

Figure 5.9
Choose Tools >
Options in
Media Player.

3. Select the Library tab, and click the Configure Sharing button (**Figure 5.10**).

The Media Sharing dialog box opens.

Figure 5.10
Click Configure Sharing.

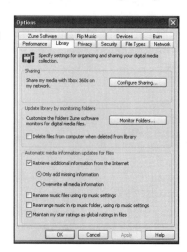

4. Click the Share My Media check box (**Figure 5.11**), and then click the OK button.

Figure 5.11
Enable media sharing in this dialog box.

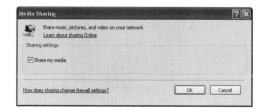

5. Reopen the Media Sharing dialog box.

You should see an see an Xbox 360 icon now
(**Figure 5.12**).

Figure 5.12
Now you have
the option to
share with your
Xbox.

6. Click the Xbox icon to activate sharing; then click
the Allow button.

When sharing is set, a green check mark appears
on the Xbox 360 icon (**Figure 5.13**).

Figure 5.13
This icon means
you're good to
go with sharing.

7. Click the OK button to finish up.

Setting up the Xbox

Now that you've set up the PC to share information with your Xbox, you need to get your Xbox configured to receive the media from your PC. Here's how to do just that:

1. Turn on your Xbox, and log in with your profile (**Figure 5.14**).

Figure 5.14
Start by signing in on the Xbox.

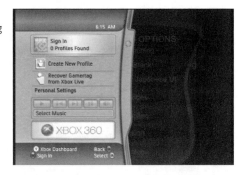

2. Go to the Media tab in the Dashboard, and choose Music (**Figure 5.15**).

Figure 5.15
Choose the Music option.

3. Choose Computer (**Figure 5.16**).

Figure 5.16
When the menu changes, choose the Computer option.

Your Zune software appears and is available to you on your Xbox 360 (**Figure 5.17**).

Figure 5.17
Now you have access to your Zune software from your Xbox.

You can sort music by albums, artists, playlists, songs, or genres, just as you can on your Zune or PC. You can also play any song you want (**Figure 5.18**).

Figure 5.18
Play any song
in your Zune
library from the
Xbox.

While a song is playing, you can turn a visualizer on
or off (**Figure 5.19**). You can even make it cover the
whole screen (**Figure 5.20**).

Figure 5.19
The visualizer
can run in a
Music Player
window...

Figure 5.20
...or fill the
screen. Groovy,
man, groovy.

Connecting the Zune to the Xbox 360

So, you don't have a network lying around that can accommodate both your PC and your Xbox 360 but still want to connect to your Zune? Well, my friend, if the stars line up properly, you can indeed connect your Zune directly to an Xbox 360 and stream songs and other media to it.

Before this can work, however, you must meet two important prerequisites:

- Your Zune's firmware must be up to date. To make sure, right-click the Zune's name on the left side of the Zune software window and choose Check for Zune Device Updates from the contextual menu (**FIGURE 5.21**).

Figure 5.21
The Zune's firmware has to be current.

- Your Xbox 360 Dashboard software must be version 2.04520.0 or later. To check, choose System Info from the Dashboard's Console Settings menu (**FIGURE 5.22**).

Figure 5.22
The Xbox 360's Dashboard software also has to be up to date.

If your Dashboard software isn't current, logging on to Xbox Live with a valid account triggers an automatic update of the Xbox 360 Dashboard software.

 Many new 360 games come with the latest version of the Dashboard software installed, and they update your Xbox automatically when you install them.

After you've tackled the software issues, you can connect your Zune to the Xbox 360 and then play your music on the Xbox. Here's a quick guide:

1. Connect the Zune to one of the USB ports on the front of the Xbox 360 (**FIGURE 5.23**).

Figure 5.23
Pick a port, and hook your Zune up to the Xbox.

2. In the Media section of the Xbox 360's Dashboard, select the Zune option that now appears there (**FIGURE 5.24**).

Figure 5.24
Choose Zune.

That's it. Now you have access to your Zune's folders (**Figure 5.25**), and you can go ahead and play media through your Xbox 360 just like you do when you're streaming from the Zune software on your PC.

Figure 5.25
Your Zune on your Xbox.

6

Accessorizing
the Zune

When most new digital media players hit the market, they usually have to duke it out for a few months before third-party companies dive in with various accessories to bolster the functionality, usability, and plain old grooviness of the device. However, Microsoft certainly got its ducks in a row by putting together an impressive lineup of accessories, most of which were ready to go the same day that the Zune hit the shelves (November 14, 2006). The upside to this is that you can go out and personalize your Zune just the way you want, adding functionality exactly as you see fit.

This chapter takes a look at what's out there as the Zune hits the ground running. But it's safe to say that by the time you read this book, there'll be plenty more Zunes pounding the pavement; therefore, you're likely to find plenty more accessories for them, too.

Case Closed

When you have a high-end piece of hardware like a Zune, the first thing you probably think of is a carrying case that serves two functions: to protect the Zune from accidents and from daily wear and tear and to reflect your personal style.

When the iPod became the "in" product to own, a huge assortment of cases and other paraphernalia appeared, but with the Zune, a great selection of cases was available from Day One. More than a dozen cases (including the one that comes with the Zune) are available in Zune.net's Accessories area.

Covering every case isn't practical, but I'll show you two or three from each category and let you decide what interests you.

What to look for in a case

This is an fairly subjective topic, of course, but most people follow some general rules in deciding whether a case is a worthwhile investment or a waste of hard-earned cash. In no particular order, the following are the things most people look for in a digital-media-player case:

- **Fashion.** If you think the Zune looks phat, you should ensure that the case you purchase for it is equally phat.

- **Attachments.** It's critical to be able to attach a case to your body or clothing. Ultimately, cases that can attach via a clip or belt loop or that fit into a pocket are the most desirable.

- **Storage.** Although any substantial storage space is going to increase the case's size considerably, having a place to store the Zune's headphones is a nice touch. Likewise, storage for the USB cable is handy but may not be practical. You have to decide where your cutoff point on storage is.

- **Access to controls.** What good is a carrying case if you can't get your hands on the controls? Don't laugh—more than a few digital-media-player carrying cases don't accomplish much besides preventing the user from accessing some or all of the device's controls. Unless telekinesis is your forte, I suggest a case that gives you easy access to controls.

- **Quality.** Obviously, something that's made well is going to last longer than something that isn't. The most important places to look for quality craftsmanship are the high-stress areas, where belt hooks or clips are attached to the case.

- **Accessibility.** Some cases lock the player up in the fashion of a bizarre, hypersecure chastity belt, making it nearly impossible to extract the device from the case without performing major surgery. For some people, this may be a desirable feature, but most everyone else will want to be able to take the Zune out of its case without too much fuss.

- **Protection.** A case should protect the player from harm, including from getting scratched and marred and perhaps even from being smashed.

The case of the hard-shell cases

Hard-shell cases are just what their name implies: cases with a hard external shell designed primarily to protect the Zune. If you drop the Zune, or if somebody shoots at you with a pellet gun, the hard-shell case is much more likely to protect the goods than a soft-shell model. The following are the most intriguing of the hard-shell cases available when the Zune came out.

Acrylic Case for Zune

Price: $29.99
Manufacturer: Belkin (www.belkin.com)

This case has highly durable acrylic sides and a metal top. Completely form-fitted to the Zune, it protects the device from any hard-core bumps or bashes. It comes with a detachable belt clip, making it easy to detach the Zune from your belt but not so easy to remove it from the case. Fortunately, the controls are fully accessible even when the case is in place.

The belt-clip portion does double duty as a kickstand-type device that allows you to prop the Zune on a table if you want to watch video content on it.

ToughSkin

Price: $34.95
Manufacturer: Speck (www.speckproducts.com)

The ToughSkin case is the big daddy of rugged cases, enveloping the Zune in a thick, rubberized shell that's an excellent choice for those who are into extreme sports or even just extreme (and messy) eating. The ToughSkin for Zune comes with a belt clip and a screen protector, so as with most other hard cases, the Zune cannot be removed without significant effort.

The other important feature is that the ToughSkin also covers and protects the buttons on the front of the Zune. You can still use the controls, however, because Speck designed the ToughSkin with overlay buttons that allow you to manipulate the controls. But be aware that the feel of the controls is going to be different with a ToughSkin in place.

Zune Gear Bag

Price: $29.99
Manufacturer: Microsoft (www.zune.net)

The Gear Bag has a semirigid exterior, but I should point out that it's not specifically a portable wear-on-your-belt bag; it's a travel pack that's portable but still holds most of your Zune paraphernalia. The bag contains space for the Zune, headphones, an AC adapter, and a sync cable. In short, it's an excellent travel pack for the Zune, allowing you to keep everything Zune-related in one spot during your trip.

tip For a greater selection of hard cases, just keep your eyes open. Searching on Google or even on eBay usually yields a nice selection of products.

Going soft

Usually more popular, soft-shelled cases come in a greater variety and provide more flexibility (both literally and figuratively) than their hard-shelled counterparts. Many soft-shelled cases are available, so I'll look at three good possibilities.

Vaja Classic Top Retro

Price: $60
Manufacturer: Vaja (www.vajacases.com)

Vaja manufactures many types of cases, and the Classic Top Retro is a prime example of its quality. The retro-design case is created with high-quality Argentine leather (or so the company says). For the executive who wants to use the Zune in style, this truly is a beautiful choice; the case's full access to controls and padded lid give it function as well as form. It's pricey, but for those who are interested in a case like this, price likely isn't an issue. The most striking thing about the Vaja case is that until you open it, you can't be sure what's inside it.

DLO Jam Jacket for Zune

Price: $19.99
Manufacturer: DLO (www.dlo.com)

The DLO Jam Jacket is a nonslip silicone skin for your Zune that fits the device snugly while keeping the screen and controls completely accessible. It's a great way to protect the Zune without breaking the bank. The downside? There's no belt clip.

Zune Canvas Sport

Price: $29.95
Manufacturer: Speck (www.speckproducts.com)

This canvas case was inspired by sneakers, according to the advertisement. That much is obvious just from looking at this case, which features a combination of rubber (on the corners) and canvas. The case has a plastic screen protector as well as access space for the controls, and the belt clip gives it utility. It's a great combination of style and function.

Sports and the Zune

The idea of having music blaring while exercising has been around since the dawn of time. Well, that's probably a slight exaggeration, but it's safe to say that the idea of having music blaring while exercising has been around for at least 50 years. The introduction of the Sony Walkman in the 1970s made it possible to take music with you everywhere, and that was the breakthrough that spurred a revolution.

The Zune is no different from other digital media players in that it makes an excellent tool for listening to content while jogging, boating, riding a bike, or engaging in any other recreational activity. The one catch is that you don't want to drop your Zune or have anything happen to it while you're bouncing around and perspiring. Fortunately, more than a few sports-related cases make the Zune easy to use on exercise day.

Sports Jacket Case with Armband for Zune

Price: $19.99
Manufacturer: Belkin (www.belkin.com)

This case is a little less over the top than the following model, because it retains more of the Zune's basic shape and is a little less shiny (both literally and figuratively). It features a tight-fitting layer of silicone rubber and a removable armband that allows you to place the Zune on your arm during exercise.

Zune Active Sport

Price: $29.95
Manufacturer: Speck (www.speckproducts.com)

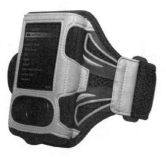

This armband truly is designed for those who want to include the Zune in their athletic endeavors. The Active Sport features breathable mesh material, reflective details (so that you can be seen at night), and adjustable Velcro straps that let you attach your Zune to your arm or other appropriate limb. This armband secures the Zune beautifully.

Travel Accessories

When it comes to travel, a few accessories stand out, the most important of which are carrying cases/gear bags and power adapters for the Zune. Fortunately, one specific "pack" of accessories is sold en masse as one item: the Zune Travel Pack.

Zune Travel Pack

Price: $99.99
Manufacturer: Microsoft (www.zune.net)

This kit takes care of pretty much all of your travel needs when it comes to the Zune. It includes five products and, therefore, has everything you need to travel away from home base:

- **AC adapter.** This adapter gives you a way to charge up your Zune without having a computer and a USB port handy.

- **Dual-connect remote.** This device lets you control playlists and other aspects of your Zune's functions. It also contains two headphone jacks with independent amplifiers, which means that you can have two sets of headphones attached to your Zune, and each listener can set his or her own volume level.

- **Premium headphones.** I'm not sure that these are necessary, because the headphones that come standard with the Zune sound fine, but these are superior, featuring an in-ear design that helps block out annoying external sounds.

- **Zune Gear Bag.** This is the bag mentioned in the cases section earlier in the chapter. It can hold all the items sold with the Travel Pack as well as the Zune itself.

- **Sync cable.** This is an extra cable that you can carry with your Zune, allowing you to connect to any computer to charge up.

note Be aware that when you're using any headphones, but especially in-ear headphones, high volume levels can lead to hearing loss over time. It's always a good idea to be cautious with volume levels when using headphones of any kind, but in-ear headphones can be especially dangerous. They are perfectly safe when used properly, of course.

TunePower for Zune

Price: $59.99
Manufacturer: Belkin (www.belkin.com)

TunePower for Zune is a portable power supply that uses a rechargeable battery (AC adapter included). Attaching TunePower to the Zune can give you up to 12 hours more play time than the Zune's battery on its own, and because TunePower comes with a stand, you can prop up the Zune on it while you watch video content.

Backup power sources like this can be very handy to have when alternative power isn't available (such as on buses, trains, or airplanes).

Car Accessories

One of the main places people use the Zune is in the car on the way to work or while ferrying kids to and from macramé classes. Although some vehicles have inputs that the Zune can plug into, many do not; therefore, you have to find a way to connect a Zune in these situations.

Two important car accessories are worth noting here, although this category is growing just as fast as every other category of Zune accessories.

Zune Car Pack with FM Transmitter

Price: $79.99
Manufacturer: Microsoft (www.zune.net)

The Zune Car Pack comes with two items: a 12-volt DC (car power outlet) charger and an FM transmitter. The transmitter allows the Zune to broadcast—wirelessly—the music playing on the Zune to your car's FM radio or stereo system. These items work in conjunction with each other, and the setting of the most suitable FM station is automatic, making the Zune Car Pack a great all-in-one vehicle system.

CarPlay Wireless Plus for Zune

Price: $79.95
Manufacturer: Monster (www.monstercable.com)

CarPlay Wireless Plus allows you to listen to your Zune wirelessly through the FM radio in your car. The bonus of this system is that it charges your Zune while it's working, so it's really a two-in-one package: a way to get your Zune's content through your car's speakers while simultaneously charging up your baby for future solo flights. It's a cool little device and well worth looking into.

Home/AV Accessories

The Zune is a great portable media device, designed primarily to be used on the road with the wind in your hair and a motorcycle vibrating between your legs. When that gets boring, however, you can connect the Zune to your home stereo or television set and show slideshows or movies, or just play music for guests at a party.

The Zune can also connect to other devices that effectively turn it into an alarm clock or ghetto blaster. This section covers a few of the key components.

Altec Lansing M604

Price: $199.95
Manufacturer: Altec (www.alteclansing.com)

The Altec Lansing M604 is a speaker set designed specifically for the Zune. This puppy has a built-in dock for the Zune and delivers surprising sound despite its relatively small profile.

The M604 comes with a wireless remote as well as built-in controls that enable you to control the Zune from afar, making this unit well worth the cost.

Zune A/V Output Cable

Price: $19.99
Manufacturer: Microsoft (www.zune.net)

The Zune A/V Output Cable allows you to listen to music through home stereo speakers or show off photos or videos on your TV screen. This cable attaches directly to the headphone jack of the Zune and then plugs into appropriate jacks in your stereo or television. Using it is simplicity itself, and it's a great way to show off a slideshow of interesting photos (such as from a recent trip to Africa) at a friend's house. You don't need to take a big photo album; instead, you can simply take the Zune and this cable and then plug directly into the nearest TV.

Zune Home A/V Pack

Price: $99.99
Manufacturer: Microsoft (www.zune.net)

The Zune Home A/V Pack comes with several key accessories that allow you to connect your Zune in numerous locations throughout your home. In my opinion, the Travel Pack, Home Pack, and Car Pack are all money well spent, although you likely don't need all three. My suggestion would be either the Home A/V Pack or the Travel Pack combined with the Car Pack.

The Home A/V Pack includes:

- **AC power adapter.** Charge your Zune without a PC.

- **Sync cable.** Synchronize your Zune with your computer.

- **A/V output cable.** Listen to music through your home stereo speakers, or show off photos and videos on a TV screen.

- **Zune Dock.** Seat your Zune in an elegant manner wherever you want.

- **Zune Wireless Remote.** This remote control is designed to be used with the Zune Dock. It gives you quick access to the current playlist as well as full control of menus and volume.

Where to Buy Accessories

Now that you have an idea of what's out there, you may want to purchase some of these fancy accessories to get your Zune purring like a kitten. Where do you go to do that? Most electronics stores, such as Best Buy (www.bestbuy.com) and Circuit City (www.circuitcity.com), carry Zune accessories, but you can also shop with confidence at Zune.net.

Check out the appendix for some online sources of Zune products.

7

Tips and Tricks

Even though the Zune hasn't been out long enough
to get really down and dirty with hidden secrets, dark
hacks, and conspiracy theories, it has plenty of cool
features that aren't mentioned often. This chapter is
the forum for that discussion. I'll show you some of
the Zune's unique and useful abilities (and how to
take advantage of them).

I'll also discuss a few hacks and mods that can alter
the way you use your Zune. These hacks are very
complicated, so I leave it to the amateur profes-
sionals online to walk you through the process. But
it's still useful to know where you can find inside
information and how-tos for those who like to tinker.

Forgotten Functions

Several important functions of the Zune are worth noting here, most of which aren't secrets. They're the kinds of things that aren't mentioned in the sparse instructions or even on many Zune-related Web sites.

Musical talents

Although the Zune is capable of holding thousands of photographs, as well as playing high-quality video material, most people are likely to start out using it as a music device. The Zune's music-management system is intuitive and functional, and a few very cool features make the Zune a most desirable device on which to enjoy your music.

Organization

The Zune and the Zune software libraries organize music in categories, making it easy to find the music you want. Those categories (listed in the Twist at the top of the screen) are:

- Songs

- Genres

- Albums

- Artists

- Playlists

When you are looking for a particular song or artist, or even for a particular style of music, these categories usually are enough. Even so, the Genres menu (**Figure 7.1**) contains nine subcategories, from Classical to Hip-Hop, so you can break your listening down even further.

Figure 7.1
The musical genres give you a chance to separate your music out by style.

Shuffle

One aspect of digital media players that makes them a big hit is their ability to shuffle thousands of songs, or a few hundred songs, or even ten songs. Whatever your taste, the ability to set the Zune to Shuffle means that you never know for sure what song is going to come up next—which, in a library of a thousand songs, means that you are always going to feel that the music is being presented in a fresh way.

You can set the Zune to shuffle through your entire music collection, within a playlist, within an album, or within a genre. Many people like to create a special playlist with several dozen to several hundred of their favorite songs and then shuffle that playlist. The result is a collection of songs that is 100 percent guaranteed to please you 100 percent of the time. You can't go wrong!

To set up shuffling so that music in any category you are playing shuffles automatically, choose Settings > Music, and set Shuffle to On (**Figure 7.2**). After that, whatever playlist you're listening to is going to shuffle its songs in random order.

Figure 7.2
All you need to do is turn on Shuffle in the Music screen.

You probably have already noticed that when you are looking at music in large categories—such as Genres, Songs, or Albums—there's a Shuffle All button at the top of every screen (**Figure 7.3**). Shuffle may not be for everyone, but for many, it's the spice of life.

Figure 7.3
You can even shuffle any major category, such as Albums.

Playlists

Playlists are lists of songs (or other audio files) you group together for one reason or another. Playlists say something about the person who makes them (see Chapter 3, which discusses celebrity playlists), but most important, they allow you to put together just the right blend of music for whatever you want. If you're having a party for people around the age of 40, for example, why not make an '80s playlist for the party? That's just the kind of flexibility that playlists afford you, and making them is well worth your time.

There are two ways to make playlists for the Zune. One method involves the Zune software (as covered in Chapter 3), and the other happens on the Zune player itself.

When you're playing a particularly engrossing song on the Zune, you can add it to the Zune player's onboard playlist, called the quick list. To add a song that you're listening to, simply click the Back button to go back to the song's title page and then click the Add to Quick List button (**Figure 7.4**). The Zune displays a "Song added" message (**Figure 7.5**).

Figure 7.4
Clicking the Add to Quick List button adds the current song to the Zune's built-in playlist.

Figure 7.5
When you've added a song, you get confirmation.

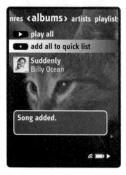

The quick-list feature gives you the power to form your own playlist on the fly, putting together a bunch of songs quickly without connecting to your PC. After you sync the Zune back with the Zune software, you can turn the quick list into a regular playlist.

tip If you want to add an entire album or an artist's whole oeuvre to the quick list, click the Add All to Quick List button instead. This feature puts the whole kit and caboodle in the quick list, but it's handy if you want to dump several albums into the Zune's built-in playlist quickly.

Sending/receiving

As I mentioned in Chapter 5, you can send songs to nearby Zune users who are within Wi-Fi range of your unit. To do this, just click the Send button below the Add to Quick List button in the song's title screen. The Zune starts searching for nearby users (**FIGURE 7.6**). When you get the Nearby list, select the person you want to send to (via the control pad) and press the OK button. The Zune sends the song to the chosen user.

Figure 7.6
When you click Send, the Zune looks for nearby Zune users to send the song to.

Conversely, if another Zune user wants to send you a song, you get a notification. Specifically, you are asked, "[Zune person] is trying to send you a song, do you want to accept it?" Press the control-pad buttons to select Yes and then press the OK button. The song is transferred to your Zune's inbox.

Blocking Out

If a particular Zune user is bothering you by attempting to send you music you don't want, you can block that user in the Community menu. I want to believe this won't happen often, but for the odd time when the situation arises, it's a nice feature to have.

To block a user, go to the Community area and choose Nearby from the Twist at the top of the screen. The next screen shows you all nearby Zune users. Select the person you want to block, click Block User, and then press the OK button.

Podcasts

Amazingly, the first version of the Zune doesn't have built-in podcasting capabilities. Even though major podcasting functions aren't available yet, you can still play podcasts on the Zune; you just have to go out and get them yourself, and then load them on the player.

Videos

When it comes to video content, note that the Zune can convert video resolution it doesn't work with to something that it can handle. If you have a movie with a resolution of, say, 640 x 400 pixels, the Zune can convert it to 320 x 240 so that it can play properly on its screen.

Another key aspect of video playback is that most videos play horizontally on the Zune, making it like a miniature widescreen TV set (**Figure 7.7**).

Figure 7.7
The Zune often plays video horizontally.

Radio

The radio feature is exceedingly simple to use. Just choose Radio from the main menu and then use the left and right control-pad buttons to find the station you want. If you want the Zune to find a station for you, press the OK button and choose the Seek option (**Figure 7.8**).

Figure 7.8
If you turn Seek on, the Zune finds the stations for you.

As I mentioned in Chapter 1, the Zune features the Radio Data System (RDS), which shows you not only the station you are listening to but also the genre of music and the song's name (**Figure 7.9**)—a cool feature, to say the least.

Figure 7.9
RDS gives you information about the station, its genre, and the song you're listening to.

Presets

Presets work just like the presets in your car radio, which is to say that a particular station becomes "married" to a button so that you can move from one station to another without scanning the entire FM band to find what you're looking for. If you are interested in placing a station in the presets list, tune to the station you want, press the OK button, and choose Add [station] to Presets.

If you want to listen to a preset station, go to the radio tuner by choosing Radio from the main menu and then press the OK button. The Zune displays your list of presets. Use the control-pad buttons to move to the station you want, and then press the OK button to select it.

tip

The Zune doesn't come with any built-in presets (how could it?), so if you want to set the presets for your area quickly, navigate through the FM band in the tuner and press OK to add the stations you want to the presets list.

There is no limit to how many presets you can set on the Zune, but if you have too many, the list can become unwieldy. Fortunately, while you scroll through the list, it wraps back to the top (or bottom) so that you can continue searching in a loop rather than going back and forth from top to bottom.

Radio Reception

You may notice that radio reception on the Zune is nonexistent if you just pick it up and try to tune in a station. If you can't get any stations, check to see whether the headphones are plugged in. On the Zune, the headphones are the only antenna; their presence or absence makes a huge difference in the quality of the FM signals that reach the device.

Pictures

Pictures are another cool part of the Zune's makeup (**Figure 7.10**). You can store a huge number of photographs on your Zune for use on the device itself, to send to other Zune users, or to connect to a television or monitor somewhere to show off a slideshow. I suppose that it won't be long before single Zune users carry around photos of themselves (perhaps even some in seductive poses) to send to Zune users they find particularly attractive. Ultimately, an entire message could be sent via a photo and a song.

Figure 7.10
You can group pictures in several ways.

Send a shot

If you want to send a particular picture to another Zune user, simply open the picture, press the OK button, and choose Send from the menu that appears (**Figure 7.11**). When you do this, the Zune searches for nearby Zune users to whom you can send the picture.

Figure 7.11
You can send
any picture
to a nearby
Zune user.

If you're interested in sending an entire folder of
pictures to another user, select the folder in question,
press OK, and choose Send from the main screen.
(The Send command appears at the top of the screen
when you're viewing pictures at folder level.)

Zoom, zoom, zoom

If you want to take a closer look at a picture, select
it and press the OK button. Then, from the menu,
choose Zoom In (**FIGURE 7.12**). The Zune zooms in on
your picture by 50 percent. You can use the control-
pad buttons to move around the picture and view it
in this close-up mode.

Figure 7.12
You can zoom
in on any
picture on
the Zune.

Slideshows

Another cool feature of the Zune is the slideshow feature. You can play any music you want behind a slideshow. To do this, follow these steps:

1. Start the music you want to use.

2. Press the Back button repeatedly until you reach the main menu.

3. Choose Pictures from the main menu.

4. Select the pictures you want to use.

   You can do this by selecting either a specific date or a specific picture folder with the control-pad and OK buttons. If you want to use all your pictures, just click Play Slideshow at the top of the Pictures screen.

5. Click the Play Slideshow button at the top of the screen to start the slideshow (**Figure 7.13**).

   The music keeps playing during the entire process.

Figure 7.13
Click Play Slideshow to get things going.

tip

When the Zune is connected to a television (via an A/V cable), you can show friends and family impromptu slideshows on a bigger screen. It's a great little entertainment medium.

The Zune shows each picture for a preset amount of time and then fades out and into another picture from the folder. To change the amount of time between pictures, choose Settings > Pictures. You can set intervals ranging from 3 to 30 seconds (**Figure 7.14**).

Figure 7.14
Set the transition time in the Pictures area of the Settings menu.

Background action

Finally, you can take any picture from the Zune's hard drive and use it as the background screen image. To do this, find a picture you like, press the OK button, and choose Apply As Background from the menu (**Figure 7.15**).

Figure 7.15
Any picture
can become
the Zune's
background
image.

Hacks

Hacking a device such as the Zune is treacherous territory. As soon as you start fiddling with registry information and altering the software (or hardware) that came with your Zune, you probably are voiding your warranty and forfeiting the right to complain if something goes terribly wrong.

Tinkering with your Zune is not for the faint of heart and should be done only if you are willing to live with lost data (songs, videos, photos) and a dead player if the hack doesn't work.

That said, many features that the Zune designers decided not to include in their player are available in other players. Not surprisingly, there are those who want those features, such as being able to turn the Zune into a portable hard drive so that it can be used to ferry files from one PC to another or perhaps to be used as a backup drive for the Zune user.

(If you want to turn your Zune into a portable hard drive, by the way, follow this link on Zuneboards—http://zuneboards.com/OFFICIAL-Use-your-Zune-as-an-External-HD-AND-ADD-FILES-t-695.html—to see the rather lengthy instructions.)

Figure 7.16
Zuneboards' discussion of how to use your Zune as a portable hard drive.

What else could possibly be done with hacks and mods to the Zune?

Check out the appendix for Web sites that contain information about other mods and hacks.

A

Zune Resources

Although the Zune just recently appeared in the marketplace, many, many Web sites are already dedicated to it. These sites offer a wealth of information and interesting dialogue among real Zune aficionados, so it can be worthwhile to drop in and see what's up.

Another reason to visit Zune sites is to find out what's coming around the corner. There's always discussion about new and exciting things, and these sites are where you can hear about them.

The sites in the second section of this appendix have cool accessories for sale.

Dedicated Zune Web Sites

http://clubzune.net

http://mszune.com

http://wiredzune.com

http://zunecorps.com

http://zuneim.blogspot.com

http://zuneinfo.com

http://zunerama.com

www.zunebuzz.com

www.zuneinsider.com

www.zunely.com

www.zunemax.com

www.zunenation.com

www.zunenewssite.com

www.zunepatrol.com

www.zunepoint.com

www.zunescene.com

www.zunesphere.com

www.zuneuser.com

www.zuneusergroup.com

www.zuney.net

Accessories Sites

www.alteclansing.com

www.amazon.com

www.belkin.com

www.bestbuy.com

www.circuitcity.com

www.decalgirl.com

www.dlo.com

www.futureshop.ca

www.griffintechnology.com/devices/zune

www.monstercable.com

www.outpost.com

www.vafresearch.com

www.zunemax.com

www.zunezag.com

www.zunezone.com

 Also check Microsoft's Zune site (www.zune.net) for news and accessories.

Index